How to
Succeed in
Real Estate...

From the People
in the Trenches
Who Do It Every Day

Michael P. Zagaris

PMZ  PUBLISHING

© 2012 by Michael P. Zagaris

Published by PMZ Publishing
1120 Scenic Drive
Modesto, CA 95350

First Printing June 2012
ISBN: 978-0-9851649-1-1

Printed in the United States of America
10 9 8 7 6 5 4 3 2 1

Library of Congress Control Number (LCCN): 2012906474

Cover design by Voltaire Victorio, PMZ Marketing Department
Photos from Shutterstock Images, LLC

Table of Contents

Acknowledgements

I have been blessed in my personal life with an extraordinary family and in my professional life by an inspiring team of real estate professionals. In these pages you will find the stories and insights of some of the dedicated agents with whom I have been fortunate to be associated.

Although I always felt I knew these folks pretty well, during the course of preparing this book I learned so much more about them and what they have to contribute. In that sense, it has been a great learning experience for me.

Time and space do not permit me to include the stories of scores of others who are equally as deserving. I am lucky to have had the opportunity to know and work with them all.

PMZ Real Estate is named after my father, Paul M. Zagaris, the founder of our company. There is no way I can ever adequately express my gratitude to him for all the learning and wisdom he imparted during his lifetime. I am also indebted to the memories of my mother, Liberty, and my brother, Steve, whose love and support I shall always cherish.

I am grateful to my partners in business: my sister, Paula Zagaris Leffler, and my brother, Jon Zagaris, for their support and leadership on a daily basis as we work together to continually transform our family business. Let me also thank my brother-in-law, Duke Leffler, for his significant contributions to our family business.

I am grateful to my partner in love and in life, my wife, Midge, for everything.

Finally, my sincere thanks go to Marc Grossman, a Sacramento writer and media consultant, who helped me shape my words and thoughts as well as the agents' stories into this book.

Introduction

Success, Happiness and a Career in Real Estate

The only security any of us has in the material world is to be found within ourselves. That is why the best investment you can make is not in real estate or stocks and bonds or any other typical investment medium, but rather in yourself. All the money or equity you may have can be lost, but no one can take away from you your knowledge and skills. And today, with unemployment rates still at distressingly high levels and the most challenging real estate market in memory, the value of having invested wisely in oneself has never been more apparent or more meaningful.

This book is written for those thinking about a career in real estate or those in the real estate brokerage community who wish to further develop themselves so they might stand out among other real estate agents as a pine tree is surrounded by willows in the forest.

When I meet men and women first entering the real estate profession, they are frequently concerned, and often insecure, about their ability to succeed. Those uncertainties typically involve anxiety about handling the technical or tactical requirements of the job. They believe mastering the preparation of contracts, the filling out of forms and learning how to handle the various steps in the transaction process are the biggest impediments to success.

Yet during my more than 30 years as the broker-owner of a real estate company, I have yet to meet a single agent who failed professionally or abandoned his or her career because he or she didn't master the technical or tactical demands. That's not to say learning them isn't important. But they aren't a major indicator of success in the profession.

What matters most and what is the subject of this book is what I refer to as the "Mental Game of Real Estate." Success is available to those who are willing to examine their own relationship with themselves and willing to change or reframe their thinking so they might both see and seize the opportunities that exist at all times, especially in times like the present when so many can't seem to see the real opportunities that abound.

So I focus in this book on three vital activities that, if embraced, will change your life.

• First, you need to prepare yourself to succeed. I use this book to share with you important practices and responsibilities that, if adopted, will set you on the course to genuine success.

• Second, you'll want to develop a compelling vision, what I call My Big Why. This book will lay out how to develop a vision of your future so powerful that it will motivate and guide you throughout your career and life, and give you a reason to get up every day to work and live.

• Finally, I will share with you a very helpful tool, what I call My Perfect Day, that will enable you to constantly remind yourself what are the most important things to do at any given time in realizing success and happiness in both your career and your life.

Let's examine each of them.

--Preparing yourself to succeed. Some agents don't understand the role of their broker. They think they are working for a broker. That's not the case. Your broker is there to provide a positive environment in which you can pursue your own self-directed journey, not as one who directs your journey—or you. You need to be your own CEO. You need to get prepared, to accept the reality that your life must be

driven by your own intentions and not by the intentions of others.

This preparation requires two essential prerequisites.

Working hard. Whether you adopt my suggestions or follow another path, you will not achieve success in your career or your life without working hard at each of them. Anyone who says you can be successful without working hard is being dishonest. There are no shortcuts. Hard work—taking care of your clients, providing outstanding service as the central means of building your client base—comes with the territory; nowhere is that more true than in real estate. Anybody who doesn't want to work hard should not get into this profession.

Being present. An indispensable ingredient to success in any endeavor, and certainly in our field, is the practice of being present in every moment of your career and life. You must focus your attention on the present moment rather than the past, the future or the countless distractions that assault us every day. It comes down to doing whatever you are supposed to be doing at the appropriate point in time. It means working when you're supposed to be working. It means spending time with your family when it's time to be with your loved ones. There is no magic formula except to just do it—now.

--Developing a compelling vision. My Big Why is all about figuring out what your intentions should be—the long-term plan of where you want to take your life. This isn't about setting an artificial goal somehow removed from yourself, something you think others want you to come up with.

It has to be a plan you buy into. My Big Why must be infused into every cell of your body. It must have a gravitational force of its own, a force in your life so powerful that you are inextricably drawn to it. It has to speak to your heart and soul, to who you are, who you want to be and where you want to be in your life.

Throughout my career, I've encouraged agents to "weave yourselves into the fabric of your community" because serving others will come back to serve you well in return. Although this is very important (and we will discuss it more later), I've become more and more convinced that agents must also "weave yourselves into the fabric of your own lives." Agents who possess clear and conscious awareness of where they are and where they want to go are best positioned to serve others and themselves.

My Big Why turns on basic elements you need to think carefully about: developing relationships, both professional and personal, so you can reach your goals; developing your career and practice in real estate to produce the resources and financial independence required to achieve My Big Why; and developing yourself so you enjoy the healthy, happy and balanced life that in the end makes it all worthwhile.

Success in your career and life demands that you learn to balance a variety of undertakings. A balanced life is one in which your focus is not solely on your career and not solely on other things. It must embrace all your relationships, your community and yourself.

Since you've decided to be in charge of your own destiny, no one else can supply My Big Why for you. Sitting down and taking the time to think about and write down My Big Why for yourself, whether it involves an hour or a day of your time or however long it takes, is the most productive exercise you will ever undertake.

My Big Why has to be special and meaningful for you. If you don't clearly see yourself in the picture of your life as you want it to turn out, you won't own My Big Why; you won't constantly strive for it and persistently transform it into My Perfect Day, an invaluable tool to accomplish the compelling long-term vision you construct.

--*Living My Perfect Day*. There are a number of planning tools available to guide you. You may discover tools on your own to adopt. That's great. This book concentrates on My Perfect Day because it is extremely powerful and easy to use. Those who employ it have generated tremendous results.

My Perfect Day will let you integrate into your life all the efforts—the activities and traits—that support you in achieving the compelling life vision you have set out for yourself. After My Big Why, sitting down and designing My Perfect Day is the second most fruitful exercise you will perform in your life.

Take your overriding goals, My Big Why, and work backwards. Ask yourself: What activities or traits do I need to adopt in the next ten years to eventually reach My Big Why? What do I need to do this year? This month? This week? This day? Make them realistic and tangible. Write them down. Use them as a kind of navigational chart or process to guide your day, your week, your month, your year. Regularly assess how you are doing in making progress—daily, weekly, monthly. Make adjustments or changes, if necessary.

My Perfect Day helps you create a practical model and valuable framework for bringing to pass those ends you identify as important in My Big Why. My Perfect Day becomes an ever-present reminder that tells you what is important to do at any given time and place. The components to consider in constructing My Perfect Day mirror the elements of My Big Why: developing relationships, a career and practice, financial independence and yourself.

All of this can be summarized very simply this way: Be prepared, decide what's important, and then make it happen. This book discusses all three components in greater depth. Each component is illustrated by the honest accounts of real-life real estate agents who are actually in the business.

That's another way this book is different. It isn't focused on some real estate guru lecturing about success or agents bragging about how great they are. Most of what you will read aren't my words; they are the stories of authentic people from all walks of life explaining in simple terms the how and why of their achievements, the personal struggles they endured to get them where they are today and how their success comes down in some way to the simple formula I've just outlined.

Finally, we try to communicate that success in your career and life can't just be judged by how many deals you make or how much commission income you earn. That's not to say those are bad things. They're just not the only things. And you won't be able to achieve them on a sustained basis without achieving balance in your life.

So this book is also about acquiring happiness in your life because if at the end you're wealthy, but not happy, what's the point? As Eckart Tolle wrote, "Gratitude for the present moment and the fullness of life now is the true prosperity."

Chapter One

Act Like a CEO

One of the biggest misconceptions people have entering real estate as an agent is the notion they are going to go to work for a real estate company. Agents need to see themselves as self-employed individuals establishing a strategic partnership with the real estate company with which they choose to work.

Those who go to work with a real estate broker thinking of themselves as employees will significantly limit their potential in the business. Unless they realize they are driving their own bus, they cannot achieve the level of success most envision when they seek out a career in our field.

Still, it is natural to assume the posture of an employee. Most people in the working world think of themselves as employees; it is what they know. Such people can take up space at a real estate brokerage firm and work in the industry, but they will never be "stars" or leaders. While a key decision for agents is which brokerage firm with which to associate, an even more important decision is how they see themselves at that company.

The challenge is for agents to see themselves as the chief executive officers, the CEOs, of their own businesses. Instead of thinking of themselves as going to work for a real estate brokerage firm, they need to say, "I'm my own boss and I'm making a strategic decision to partner with my broker."

The psychological distinctions between employees and the self-employed are momentous. They make all the difference in being successful over time.

If you genuinely embrace the notion that you are a self-employed individual and the CEO of your own business, you are simultaneously accepting responsibility for your own fate and future. Contrast that concept with those who view themselves as employees, who perceive themselves as individuals following the instructions of others, as men and women whose fates and futures are dictated by how well they serve their superiors.

It is all about mindset. If you think you are the boss and the future is in your hands, then you recognize your real estate broker as a strategic partner and not as an employer. If that is the case, you are well positioned to take advantage of the ample opportunities this career presents. There is still much hard work ahead, but you have taken the first big step to success.

You're the boss. You may succeed or fail. But you're going to do it by yourself.

There are also significant legal and tax differences between being an employee and being a self-employed person. You are required to pay both sides of Social Security; forward all state and federal taxes, usually on a quarterly basis; and separate personal from business income and expenses in order to properly take business deductions.

Okay, now you realize you are self-employed and not taking directions from someone else.

This doesn't mean real estate is easy. It is a serious undertaking. Nobody is going to develop a plan of action or a path to success for you.

The education agents receive in order to obtain their real estate license is important, but it is largely unrelated to the skills they require to be successful real estate practitioners. The learning directed at getting a license primarily concentrates on issues of concern to the state real estate licensing agency. The government wants to be sure agents know how to conform to the myriad state laws governing real estate. Such instruction is less focused on the actual practice of real estate per se: what it takes to mount a successful career, seek out and develop a clientele and work effectively with people.

This leads to a fundamental misconception among some agents who have recently earned their licenses: They think they know how to perform in real estate. It's not necessarily true. Receiving their real estate licenses merely means they have the knowledge required to pass the state test.

Therefore, it is important that all real estate professionals embrace a life-long learning process early in their careers. At our firm we make available to all agents a comprehensive in-house training process. It features an eight-week long orientation course for new agents as well as ongoing classes every day of the week on a host of practical topics for both new and experienced sales professionals. We offer an extensive lending library of training materials on every possible area of interest to our agents. Additionally, we identify and promote numerous outside sources of continuing education for agents, from community colleges and universities to specialized authorities within the industry who regularly sponsor seminars.

In summary, if you're going to be your own boss, you need to create your own plan, execute it and monitor the results. This is what accepting responsibility is all about. Going into real estate isn't easy. It requires maturity. No one's going to make you do what it takes to be successful except yourself. You have to be a self-starter.

I have stressed the importance of being your own boss, but this doesn't mean you have to re-invent the wheel, starting from the beginning and learning the essential lessons of the business the hard way, by trial and error. Today's agents can benefit from the experiences of successful practitioners who have come before.

Any number of productive PMZ agents qualify as successful practitioners. Here are just a few of their stories in their own words.

~

AARON WEST
'One of the last true entrepreneurial businesses'
(Aaron West is as disciplined in athletics as he is in his real estate business dealings.)

I was born in Quincy, California, up in the Sierras above Oroville, in 1970. My dad spent his whole life in sales and management. My mom stayed at home with us kids, of which I'm the oldest of six. We moved around a good little bit, living in Idaho for a while and in Reno for a good bit. I went to high school in Willows, 90 miles north of Sacramento.

I didn't really know what I wanted to do growing up. Did a little bit of college. Realized most of my friends who graduated with marketing degrees were waiting tables or doing nothing with what they learned in college. I was fortunate in that my grandfather and my dad had a good amount of people skills. I knew whatever business I ended up in would involve dealing with people.

I worked in my early 20s tinting auto windows for a company in Reno. In 1995, I went to work for the Rogers Jewelers chain at a small store in Reno. I did really well there. In '97, they transferred me down to the Modesto store, where I remained in sales. I enjoyed a really good career with Rogers. It's a great company that takes good care of its employees. I was top salesman for the whole chain from '99 until '04. I was with the company for 10 years and really liked it. But one problem with a company that hires well and takes good care of employees is it has very low turnover. So I figured I'd gone as far as I could. For the money I was making and the time I was there, there were not a whole lot of stores I could take over. But I had started a family and didn't want to move far away from Modesto.

In 2005, I was talking to my father-in-law, who had been a real estate broker in Reno. "I wouldn't wish real estate on anybody," he told me. But in the next breath he said, "You need to get into real estate because it's a very challenging career. There's no one to hold you accountable. You're interacting with people all day long. You have to be able to deal with every personality there is out there. And you have to be a self-starter, for all intents and purposes, with different cycles—so there is a very low success rate for real estate professionals." He added, "It's a very front-end loaded business; the longer you're in real estate, the better your reputation becomes, the more business that comes to you and the easier it comes to you."

His advice rang true. It was consistent with what I knew working in retail when I was with Rogers in the jewelry stores. If I worked hard, success would just come. I was fairly self-confident. I knew my skill- sets pretty well. For me, real estate wasn't a matter of reinventing the wheel. Real estate is one of the last true entrepreneurial businesses there are. There are so many different people from every walk of life who are successful at it. Eighty percent of real estate agents don't last three years, but I thought if you work hard and smart, you couldn't help but succeed.

I got my real estate license after taking the test. I knew from the retail years with Rogers that my goal was to go to a brokerage company that had some brand recognition and strength. I went to the top three companies in Modesto, sitting down and talking with their recruiters. I met with Matt Keenan, who was a client of mine at Rogers. I called him because I knew he worked as a recruiter for PMZ. Just like I did at the other two companies, I asked Matt if I could speak with Mike Zagaris, the owner of PMZ. Twenty minutes after speaking with Matt, I got a call from Mike and we proceeded to have a 30- or 45-minute conversation about real estate, what PMZ had to offer and what PMZ was doing. It was the peak of the market at the time. Everyone was rolling in money. Prices were so high that homes were selling quickly.

My dad raised me to be a businessman who owns a real estate company, just like Mike Zagaris. One of the things I found about most people in sales is they're not necessarily good business people; they're good sales people. So someone who comes from a sales background and becomes a businessperson can become a good one. But someone who is a businessperson first is going to make business decisions first. I knew Mike Zagaris would always take care of the people who did business, who sold houses. I knew he would make business decisions based on things that make business sense and not necessarily on the basis of emotion.

Another thing that impressed me about Mike was he talked about the market and what he saw coming, and he knew, as I did, that there would be a change. It was at a point when there was way too much chaos, frenzy and craziness. Everybody was buying, selling and investing. That's not how the world works for too long. Those kinds of booming markets can't go on indefinitely. One of the things that's different about PMZ and its people is most other companies and agents are spending every penny they get; at PMZ we put away money because the market is going to change. My goal is when it does change and everybody else is running scared, we'll be in a position to grow this company.

I started with PMZ in 2005, and worked my tail off. I decided how I would do business. I had one easy sale before the market turned. It listed and sold in one day with multiple offers. Shortly after that the market turned into the real market we're in today. My first six months I sold three houses. I wasn't discouraged because I knew I was building my business the right way. I started with a little bit of a database from my clients with Rogers who trusted how I did business.

I knew the way to build a business was by doing it with people I knew or whom I had met and created relationships with. I also decided to get a business coach, to help hold me accountable and keep me on track. As a triathlete, I learned a coach may not change your whole approach but can give you an outside perspective that keeps you on point.

My business has just gained momentum and gained momentum and gained momentum by consistently doing the same thing—

producing for my clients—over and over and over again. That's how I gained traction. I went from three homes sold during my first six months to 19 the next year to 29 in the next year to 49 the next—and to 60 in the last year.

My sales are going up despite the housing market collapse. Markets like these are what are called a professional's market. A turkey can fly in a hurricane. When the market is going crazy good, it doesn't matter who you are—whether or not you know how to sell a house. It doesn't matter. In a down market, people aren't so willing to trust their brother, cousin or nephew who is working as a novice part-time real estate agent. They want a proven professional who has made this a career and has a system in place to get the job done.

One conscious decision I made when the market turned was not to represent banks. The majority of professionals in this market went to banks for listings because they understood banks would be a really good client that could regularly supply listings, primarily from foreclosed properties, during the five- or six-year period before the market turned around again. The problem I saw with this strategy is that when the market turns again, and it will because real estate is cyclical, agents who over-rely on banks will find their one or two or three clients will disappear, and these agents will have to rebuild their businesses from nothing because they have no other clients.

Instead, I decided to work with real people in this most difficult of markets. So I mostly represent buyers and the real sellers who are out there. I've put together a solid set of systems so every client gets treated the same way and has the same experience.

Any time anybody is referred to me, which is where most of my business comes from, I don't show any houses until the client is pre-approved by their lender so they know what they qualify for. Next, we have a 45-minute to one-hour conversation in my office about the market, what they can expect from it, what's the best scenario for them in purchasing a home and what they should expect of me and what I will expect of them. So there are clear expectations on both sides as we move forward.

This system gives people realistic expectations about the market. There's so much misinformation about what happens on a daily basis in real estate from everywhere: from neighbors to media outlets to people you meet at the store. Sitting down and having things clearly explained helps clients know what the actual state of the market is today. After all, for the past five years, there's a different market every two months. What people heard five months ago is not relevant to what's going on now. So explaining what's going on, the process of finding a home and the value I bring to the table helps clients understand why I may not do what they hear other agents do.

This is probably the most important thing real estate agents can do when they start working with clients: Take the time to understand what's important to clients so agents can help look out for their best interests. I ask them, "What do you expect of me as your real estate agent?" because I want to hear from them what they want to happen. My favorite quote in business is, "At the root of all conflict is the violation of expectation." I don't know where I heard that. But it makes so much sense to me. In any divorce or other conflict, one person expects the other person to do something and vice versa. And it all blows up because they didn't have clear and mutual expectations. I want to understand their expectations of me so I can address those issues. And I want to let them know what I expect of them so we have a good relationship moving forward.

A real estate agent is a facilitator. I'm like a wedding planner; I'm not necessarily the guy who will find them their house, but once they find it, I'm the one who will help them get that house and make for a smooth process to get in it. I tell my clients that for me the best case scenario is at the end of the process they look back and say, "He didn't really do that much." That means I did my job right. There is no such thing as a smooth escrow; there are always problems going on with the bank or someone else. My job is to take all of those problems off their hands. If there's a problem I can't handle by myself, I approach them and find a solution. I take on as much of the pressure and dilemmas on myself because there's already enough stress involved in buying a home.

The other thing I tell clients is that real estate is my career, but I'm not a perfect real estate agent. If I'm not doing something to their expectations, I ask them to give me the courtesy of telling me before they go get another agent. If they're not happy with me I want to have the opportunity to fix it or explain why I'm doing something in a certain way. This allows clients to show me some grace. I also may not be doing something right for my other clients, who may not say anything. And that's not acceptable to me.

In our business, in a market like this, 8 percent of the agents do 92 percent of the business. The difference doesn't involve the big things. Everybody knows how to write up a contract and sell a house. The difference is being able to consistently do the little things—the things that separate the true professionals from the vast majority of agents.

Another thing that makes a difference for me at PMZ is that Mike, as a figurehead and owner, truly does have an open-door policy with all of his agents. He takes the time to respond when someone asks him a question or asks for a meeting or to go to lunch. I've been fortunate to go to lunch with him on any number of occasions. He always makes the time, which genuinely separates him from most of the rest of the real estate companies. He is extremely open to helping out agents. Many times I've had an issue or question about the market or I have to make some really hard business or personal decisions involved in making my business grow. He's always extremely open and accessible, and willing to talk or help.

∼

DANIEL DEL REAL
'Controlling my own destiny'

(A young husband and first-time father, Daniel Del Real also juggles a successful career in real estate. He was named by Realtor® Magazine as one of the top 30 agents under the age of 30 in 2010.)

My parents, life-long real estate investors, got me into real estate after I served four years in the military. Once into it, I never looked back.

I was born in 1981 in San Jose, California. My dad is now retired but was a factory worker at the Hilmar cheese company in Hilmar, California, south of Modesto. We moved there in 1989 and I went to junior high and high school there.

At age 17, I knew exactly what I wanted to do: law enforcement. The first thing I did after turning 18 was sign papers to go into the military—to become a military police officer in the Air Force. I was also attending community college full time and earned an A.A. degree in criminal justice. I had a job lined up with the Santa Clara Police Department.

It all changed for me when I got out of the military in 2003. I always had these conversations with my mom, who is first generation American. My parents always had rental properties. Because of language barriers, during the 1980s and '90s my siblings and I helped them with lease and purchase agreements, and loan documents.

Their first investments were in the Bay Area. Then in the late '80s and early '90s, they started buying mostly in Modesto. It made more sense. The properties there were cheaper and they could realize more cash flow.

So I kind of knew what my parents did, their sources of income coming mostly from the rentals. Every time I came home on leave from the military, we sat down and talked real estate. My mom nudged me into real estate, introducing me to a real estate agent friend and encouraging me to talk with him. It didn't take much. My biggest fear was to give up all I had already done to pursue a dream in criminal justice; I had met all my goals to be in law enforcement. I was afraid to take the risk and didn't even know what to do to get a real estate license. But the agent reassured me: "You already know real estate. You're a natural. It's not that hard [to get licensed]. It's a matter of taking a few classes."

"I'll give it a shot," I replied. I didn't waste any time. I came home from the Air Force on a Thursday in October. By the following Monday I was already going to my first class. I wanted to get in and see if I liked it or not.

So my mom convinced me to go into real estate as a career. I look back over the last six or seven years, and it's been full steam ahead in real estate.

Once my classes began, I started to get to know a lot more about the industry. I also talked more with my parents about their real property investments and what they had achieved. That's where my interest came from in the beginning. I learned that the sky is the limit. What I didn't realize then was that I could also control my own destiny. I was used to the structure, structure, structure of the military. Being my own boss was foreign to me after that. But what really got to me was sitting down with my mom and dad and reviewing the investments they made. My dad never went past junior high school; my mom never made it past the third grade. With pretty much no education, they were working minimum-wage jobs. They certainly didn't have high paying jobs.

My dad was making $35,000 a year from his job and supporting five kids: four boys and a girl. After sitting down with my mom and dad, I saw they were making another $4,000 a month just from rental income.

I didn't know what to expect or how much money I would make in the real estate industry. What drove me was seeing my parents and wanting to be where they were when I am their age through hard work together with good investments—to do as they had done. I was like a sponge, soaking up learning about the ins and outs of real estate. The classes opened up my eyes. From there I took off and never looked back. After six years in the business, I think I have as many rental properties now as my parents built up after 20 years.

After passing the class, I got my license. I was sort of afraid about what to do next.

I didn't know many people. I was 22 years old. I thought it would be difficult starting off because of my young age—that buyers and sellers would question how long I had been in the industry. Fearing that would be an obstacle, I knew I had to soak up everything, learn as much as I could about real estate and investments to overcome the objection.

First, there was just reading. I read almost every book I could get my hands on about real estate. Then I looked at blogs and websites, focusing on everything I possibly could to become more familiar with the industry.

Then I learned by doing. I started getting busier. I learned from two seasoned agents at PMZ, Joseph Bondi and Chris Shaw, the biggest agents in the office. They took me under their wings and gave me the confidence to move forward.

When I started working and people started seeing I knew what I was doing and doing the right things for my clients, my client and referral base grew. Everyone in real estate says to stay in touch with your clients. We used to do that because not everyone has developed new generation buyers like I have. I still send personal notes to old clients. I also send personal notes to new generation clients.

∿

LORRAINE CARDOZA
'Service-driven' and 'client-obsessed'
(An experienced agent before moving to Modesto, Lorraine Cardoza has been very successful at PMZ Real Estate.)

I had been a licensed agent working in the Midwest until coming here in mid-1996 and joining PMZ in 1997. I see people in this company who are so disciplined and structured. Mike Zagaris is really into prospecting. I had never done business that way before. He said to go out and prospect.

People would say they do prospect from eight to ten in the morning and from one to four in the afternoon. They would put prospecting in their schedules and do it religiously. I had never done that. I always took every opportunity to build my business, gave the best I had to offer and hopefully that would lead me down the road to more business.

That's how I built my business two other times. It takes longer, but the benefits come back strong.

I prospect every day of my life. And I always make sure people know what I'm doing. But I don't pick up the phone and make cold calls, with all due respect to other agents who do.

My business is really service-driven. It is client obsessed. I want to make sure clients have everything they need. In a relatively short time, I have built up a very good business doing exactly that. I expect it to go on and on and on because my base is always getting bigger.

The first year I was here Mike wanted an actual plan. I was beside myself in assembling one. Someone in the office helped me put the numbers together.

I thought they were too low. But it made me conscious about how important it is for me to write out my goals in terms of what I want to accomplish each year: personal, financial and others. I'll set that goal and more often than not make or exceed it.

Up on the board in my office I have posted my goals and below them what I'm doing in terms of units so I can look at them every day. I know I want to save X amount of money a year and do X amount of dollars every year in volume. The volume of gross sales drives me. That's the accumulated total of the sales prices of everything I sold in the year.

When you talk with agents and ask what their goals are this year, you will get one of three answers, in my opinion: sell X amount of units, make X amount of money or achieve X volume of gross sales.

There is no one right answer. I want to do volume. Someone else will use units sold. I don't care what agents write down as long as they are writing their goals. When I begin each day I internalize my goal; achieving that goal becomes an unconscious ongoing process. And when you make it happen, you succeed.

There are so many things to do to make things work right when you are taking care of a client. At first I have a checklist. When the checklist is no longer necessary, when it becomes part of what you do and who you are, things become much easier. It becomes part of your personality.

When my husband and I lived in a Chicago high-rise, we'd get in the elevator and before reaching our floor, everyone in that elevator knew what I did. The greatest thing was that I was doing it unconsciously; I didn't have to think about it. I wasn't uncomfortable doing it.

When I speak to classes of new agents at PMZ University, I stress the fact that people can't do business with you unless they know what you do.

Now I have a licensed assistant and she can make extra income by referring clients to me. You either have the ability to do that or you don't. It doesn't mean you can't be an agent if you don't have it. You just have to do it consciously then, almost get a script, memorize it and remember to use it every chance you get.

Someone at the PMZ University class asked how I get things done. I replied using the story of how when we lived in Chicago my husband would always laugh at me because when we got in an elevator or entered a restaurant, I would say, "Wow, what a day. I sell real estate and some days are rough (or easy)." It gives you the opportunity to tell people what you're doing.

The point is that you have to be the driver to create business opportunities. Once you have those opportunities, you need to do something with them; they have to take root.

It takes two; you have to show the client you will take care of them better than anyone else. You do that by actually taking care of them better than anyone else.

For most people, even if they've bought or sold a house before, it's still a big deal. It is their biggest investment. I don't care if the person is a first-time buyer or someone handling major properties. He or she deserves the respect of being treated like it is a big deal.

That means answering questions, getting back to them with requested information, providing a prompt response on offers. They need to be confident you've got their best interests at heart and you're implementing a plan to help them achieve their goal.

I believe my success has been all about service.

You also need to have the old fire in the belly. I was on tour with a gentleman who had been selling real estate for a while. I asked what he thought it takes to be really successful in this marketplace. He answered that you need to have lived here all your life. I replied that I hoped he was wrong or I didn't have a shot in hell.

I don't think that's what it takes. There are people in our industry who have lived here forever who don't do a hill of beans worth of business. And there are those who do phenomenally well and haven't lived here forever.

Those people who can't possibly see themselves not succeeding don't fail. I can't imagine not succeeding, even though I can't give you the A, B, C and D of what it takes to succeed. It's a mindset. It is the old adrenalin rush to just get up and go.

~

PAUL HARMON
'Thinking outside the box to stay on the cutting edge'
(His mom, Pam Harmon, is one of the top-performing agents at PMZ and Paul has followed in her footsteps. He is now PMZ's vice president of strategic initiatives.)

I was born in 1973, in Modesto. My mom always helped my dad in his building contractor business. But her biggest priority was my younger sister and I. It wasn't until I was 12 that she got into real estate and became one of the top real estate agents in Stanislaus County. She was named Realtor® of the Year for 2009 out of 2,200 potential candidates in the county.

I grew up together from the first grade with Ben Balsbaugh, now a vice president of residential sales at PMZ. We had a great childhood. I was exposed to so many different cross-sections of people. One of my dad's practices was to always get me to be with adults from a very young age. I think he saw the value in exposing me to different mindsets and viewpoints. His thought was that if I wasn't sheltered, I would be stronger and more effective at whatever was my chosen field—and he also wanted to expose me to a multitude of different fields.

That's important to keep in mind as you get older. It's easy to retreat into your comfort zone. So it's important to continue challenging yourself, which means exposing yourself to different things. One of the greatest attributes Mike Zagaris passed on to me is being progressive. I interpret that as always evolving, as individuals and as a company. At PMZ, we don't dismiss others' viewpoints; we take them in, process them, argue and debate over them, and flush them out. It's an exercise we do all the time. I like to debate, to argue. Playing both sides, being the devil's advocate, is a trait that has developed in me.

From an early age, I remember sitting on the couches of homes we visited. I'd ask people to talk about their successes and failures. I always tried to get out of them the things they would do the same and what they would do differently. That's how I would learn from their experiences. Surprisingly, few people, especially ones my age back then, would ask such questions. At first, many people were a little taken aback. It means they had to drop their guard and expose themselves. But when they saw I valued and respected their lives, opinions and viewpoints, most opened up. They weren't just canned questions. I'd say, "I can see you had a lot of successes in your life. How were you able to accomplish them? How would you do things differently?"

My parent's view was each generation should be better than the previous generation. So they encouraged my sister and I to think outside the box, to push beyond what had been their limits.

I grew up in the country. My family had an almond ranch. When I was eight years old, in fourth grade. I remember when three-wheeler motorbikes came out. As a country boy, I wanted one. They cost $3,000. I vividly recall my dad saying, "If you earn half, I'll put up the other half." I knew I was going to earn that half. This was right before school let out. That summer, I came up with a plan to earn the $1,500. I mowed lawns, did yard work, painted fences—any and all odd jobs I could do.

The problem is when you live in a rural area, there are not a lot of target markets for such labor. Roads are rough, and I recall pushing the lawnmower and wearing out the wheels so my dad had to keep replacing them. I remember finally coming to him with my $1,500 at the end of summer.

"What's this?" he asked.

"This is the money, the money for the three-wheeler," I answered. As I handed it over to him, he counted it.

"Let's go," he said. We went directly to the motorcycle shop and bought it right then. At that point I knew I could always make money. If I had a clear vision, I could accomplish it. This is only one example of how my dad knew to motivate me. He knew to put something out there for me to achieve and I would rise to the challenge.

I grew up inspired by both my mom and dad along with sports, family, friends and church, graduating from Modesto Christian High School. Both my parents had extremely hard work ethics.

As I got a little older, starting around 11 or 12, I worked during summers for my father's construction company. I came to run construction crews at custom homes or commercial sites. Being there and managing men had its difficulties because of my young age and because I was the boss's son. But my dad threw me in there anyway.

I didn't like construction for a number of reasons. Much of the time you are dealing with trades people who don't run their businesses like a business, but like a trade. It's always a battle when you're trying to get jobs done profitably. One of my dad's main objectives was to give me the chance to see that I didn't like construction. "Son," he told me, "you go out, you get an education and experience. If you want to come back and run this business, you can always do so."

The overriding vibe in my family was unconditional love with safety nets. My parents would push and push us to go out and try new things, knowing they were always there for us. We always had a place to come back to.

I attended California State University, Stanislaus, graduating with in 1996 with a B.S. degree in business administration, marketing and management. I also met my future wife, Meika, in college. We were married in 1999.

It was my senior year in college, with one semester to go before graduating. I was going crazy, seeing all these people making money in business. I called up my dad: "I'm done. I've got enough knowledge. I'm going to quit school and go out on my own."

"Okay, no problem," he replied. "Let me call you right back."

He called my mom and asked her what I owed for all of the schooling they'd been covering. When I was younger, in high school, he would say, "Whatever you start, you finish. I don't care if you don't like it or do it the next season, but you finish the season or whatever it is."

So my dad called me back, as promised: "No problem, son. Just swing by with a check for [I don't remember how many tens of thousands of dollars] for four years of college." He knew my number. The reason I was quitting college was to make money. So if I didn't finish, it would cost me a lot of it. So quitting wasn't a smart business decision.

"I get it, dad," I said. And I completed college.

Before finishing, during the summer before my senior year, I was working on one of my dad's construction sites. He was building a house for a business executive in town. I built some rapport with this CEO, asking in typical fashion how he became successful. I told him I was looking to do an internship the following spring. He didn't have any, but I was persistent and he developed one. So I became a marketing representative for this athletic footwear manufacture, flying around the country visiting all the Foot Lockers and Kenny's shops—all the big-name stores. I was actually called a tech rep. All I was there to do was to describe how the shoe of my company was the best shoe they could buy. I educated everyone on the shop floor how to sell the shoe.

I felt like a rock star, jet-setting around the U.S. with an expense account and having a lot of fun. I negotiated a position with the company as marketing brand manager for a line of its shoes and continued flying extensively around the country for the next several years.

As always, I asked people, colleagues in the company, about what they were doing and how things worked. As I looked at the vice presidents who served above me, I noticed they were all divorced or on their second or third marriages. They were always missing their kids' games and usually not enjoying much of a successful home life. I looked into the future at this company and saw that it wasn't for me.

I was getting ready to be married to Meika. (We now have twin boys, eight years old, and a ten-year-old daughter.) What I was doing wasn't the way to establish a great home life, I concluded. So I decided to go do what I knew. I knew about construction and real estate. I went to work for ReMax, a Modesto real estate firm. I saw myself as the next generation of Realtor®.

The way I saw it was that unfortunately, most real estate agents don't treat their job as a business. So they don't have degrees, marketing plans, strategies or much discipline. My view was if you come into an industry where you know a lot of people, where you have a plan and are able to finish and execute, you could be successful. I saw my dad and mom's hard work and discipline and saw the fruits of their labors. I knew real estate was always something that could be very lucrative.

My mom has a lot of heart. For her, real estate was absolutely not just about the sale; it was about getting kids into houses. Clients were always part of our Christmas and Thanksgiving celebrations. I enjoy that aspect of it too, but I also enjoy the aspect of the work from a business standpoint. I thought I would work more with business professionals and investors, and not necessarily first-time homebuyers.

In 1998 and '99, the market was healthy. I set out after it. My aim was to go after the young professionals in Modesto, investors who would want a young, aggressive entrepreneur representing them versus someone who was not as progressively businesslike. Clients want to deal with people they like, respect and who are like themselves. I figured I'd go after their business by being the kind of real estate professional I would want for myself. I saw a void among the agents in the Modesto market.

I knew so many people in Modesto from my family. But I didn't want anyone to think since I'm a second generation Realtor® that I was getting business because of my last name. And I didn't want my mom to feel I was poaching on her clientele. That added some new challenges.

I can still remember when I tapped into the Latino market. My first 20 homes sold in the Latino community came through one family I linked up with. That got me going.

It's all about your referrals and sphere of influence. If you sell the father a house, do a good job and maintain the relationship, years later you might sell the daughter or son a house, too. I probably grew up with that son or daughter, but I didn't want my mom to think I was appropriating the relationships she had nurtured over time.

After five or six years of success at Re-Max, I got a call from Ben. I knew of PMZ and how strong and progressive Mike was. PMZ's web site is what they're all about. I found my own clients going to its web site to find houses I hadn't supplied them. "Don't worry, Paul," my clients said to me. "We'll use you; you're our guy. But PMZ's site is so superior."

I took over PMZ's operation on Carpenter Road. This is where my business side helped me from a leadership standpoint. I'm not necessarily a sales person. Real estate is a commodity for me. I'm a businessperson, and real estate happens to be my profession.

Since taking over the Carpenter Road operation. I've overseen $1.5 billion in transactions. It's grown from 60 agents to now about 110.

My Big Why is being an integral part of the leadership at PMZ and transforming real estate in the Central Valley. How as a company do we continue to be progressive and be on the cutting edge, but also not necessarily go along with the herd? Social media. The Internet. Those are great. But if you're not inspiring people to use them, it's all for naught.

At the end of the day, it's all about faith, your family and your fulfillment, which will be different for everybody. Now I'm trying to think about how I'm going to inspire my kids and create that legacy. Going back to my parent's vision of the next generation being better than the previous one, I've got to equip and provide my children with some pretty great tools that will allow them to do better than I did.

～

MATT KEENAN
'A step of faith'

(A former truck driver, Matt Keenan has been in the real estate business for several years and has developed a highly successful practice. Today, Matt serves as director of recruiting at PMZ.)

I'm a high school graduate from Manteca who drove trucks for 15 years before entering real estate.

Mike Zagaris said I would be able to do it. I thought he wanted me to fill a spot at the desk like the other brokers I interviewed with. But my first experience when I started this venture was a lot of nervousness and fear.

The manager of my old trucking company called and asked how real estate was going. "Terrible," I replied. My old manager said he had a spot open at my former company and I accepted.

So I had all my stuff packed up and was ready to go back to driving trucks. I went by Mike's office and told him, "I appreciate the opportunity to give the real estate profession a shot. It's just not working out. I haven't sold anything in the last few months. I need to provide for my family so I'm going to quit."

He told me to come in and close the door. "What if I met with you once or twice a week?"

"I don't know if that will really help," I said.

"Once a week let's go over building your plan," Mike urged.

After spending a month going over things with Mike and putting into place what he was telling me, I put eight or nine homes into escrow. It wasn't so much what Mike said to me but the fact he went the extra mile to help me make my business a success. I thought to myself, how could I quit on someone who isn't quitting on me?

Mike and I kept meeting. He told me I have to start reading: Business Week, Forbes magazine. He started giving me his old magazines when he was through with them.

Now I'm teaching classes for new agents at PMZ University, which humbles me. Management asks me to teach courses on listing presentations, how to present myself to sellers and how to help them choose me to sell their homes. I repeat a motto I heard long ago: People don't care how much you know until they know how much you care.

I've beaten a lot of more seasoned agents out of properties by simply going and listening carefully to sellers talk. I listen to their concerns, what they're looking for. When someone puts their home on the market, many agents out there don't care about helping them find a place to go. They just care about putting their sign up on the seller's lawn.

One thing that has helped me is that I won't go into a listing presentation by just talking about what their home is worth and how I can sell it. I go into that presentation by finding out where they want to go and what they are looking for in a new home: size, area, amenities and price. Then they see I really care about their needs.

It's the truth. I do.

It can be frustrating and very personal when sellers talk to agents about the homes they fixed up and put all this sweat and energy into.

My clients know I care where they are going and my job is to help them find a place where they can feel comfortable raising a family. It isn't just about sales; it's about helping people get what they want. I try not to be pushy with people; I just try to help.

When you push too hard and try to make quick sales, you don't get that long-term repeat business. Then you're in this business for the short haul. But if you can get people to realize you honestly and sincerely care about their needs and you're not just trying to make a dollar, you get that repeat referral business.

During my first two years in business I spent a lot of time—three to four hours a day—prospecting for-sale-by-owners, what they call FSBOs. I'd go online to pull up local newspapers, copy the FSBOs and paste in the numbers for the do-not-call list. Certain people don't want to be called so I don't call them. But I might drop by and knock on their doors. Others who weren't on the do-not-call list I'd definitely call. I still do it. I just got another for-sale-by-owner by calling; it's already in escrow.

I don't think I took a day off during my first year when I was building my business. I worked seven days a week. After that I started taking some days off. But that first year I wanted to be sure I was available to anybody who needed me. It worked well. In the first eight months after I started meeting with Mike I sold 36 homes. The second year I sold 44 homes. This past year I sold 54.

It keeps on getting bigger and bigger with less legwork because now I'm getting referrals. That doesn't mean I don't have to ask for referrals. People will forget about you if you don't ask. I tell people, "By the way, if you know anyone else looking to buy or sell, please don't hesitate to give them my name and number."

Now I get more business with that little phrase than by three or four hours spent prospecting every day. I'll call past clients. Or when I'm prospecting for-sale-by-owners, if I feel like I've made a connection with someone on the phone, I'll ask.

I get cards or letters from people who say, "You're real nice and if I ever think of buying or selling, I'll give you a call." Sometimes when you prospect, you may not hear from someone in eight or nine months. Then they call and say, "It's time my wife and I want to sell." I just closed one like that.

It's like planting a seed. It can take a long time for the plant to grow. I also call people periodically during the year with information. I'll say, "I don't know if you're aware of this, but a home came up on the market just a few blocks from you. It's comparable and is listed for X." Sometimes that piques people's interest.

Sometimes they'll say, "We're interested but we're just not there yet." I say, "Fine, whenever I can help you get where you want to go, please keep me in mind." When they're ready, they'll call.

You don't get all of them, but your chances sure increase by staying in touch.

Your plans change from year to year. My first plan was to just call and prospect. Different agents are better at different things. My thing is I'm good on the phone. Others like to do it with open houses. I've done that too. But now I value my weekends and taking time with family. Other people are better in person than I am. You have to find your strength and emphasize it.

The way you find that area of strength is by experimenting: phoning, open houses, walking neighborhoods, going door to door, dropping off flyers. At the door it's a real quick conversation: "I just want to let you guys know I just sold a house right around the corner from you."

I personally find it's always easier to sell to someone when I act like I don't care about the sale. I act as if I have all the money in the world. It's like when you're dating a girl and don't want to be too pushy. You want to romance the clients a little bit. That lets the clients know you care more about them than making the sale.

I don't come up to clients and throw a contract in their faces and say "Sign here!" They want to get to know me first. I don't want to go into business with someone who doesn't know me.

So I talk about myself a little bit. I explain who I am, what my philosophy is, how long I've been in business, how long I've been married, the number of kids I have and how I got started in real estate.

Actually, people like to talk about themselves more. So if I can get them to do that, they feel more comfortable with me. The majority of the time it works better when your clients can talk about themselves more than you talk about yourself. If you do that, you will be very successful.

It can be a little hard. Sometimes people don't want to talk. I keep on asking questions like I'm interested, not like I'm performing on stage. And the fact is, you have to really be interested in your people.

My business plan has changed. After a year of not taking time off and prospecting three to four hours each day—with every weekend spent at open houses and walking neighborhoods—I started building up a contact list. Then I would be prospecting people I already knew. For example, at the door I'd ask, "How's your home? How are you enjoying it?" I would not sit down. It would be a quick talk and then I'd leave. It was usually not more than 10 minutes. But after the conversation was finished and the visit was ending, I'd ask for referrals.

You care more about your company when you're not being paid by the hour. You care more about doing a thorough job and completing it. When I was driving trucks for a living, I put everything into it as well. I don't like to do things half way.

That's why my old boss at the trucking company was asking me back. I drove a mountain route. I was picking up and delivering. I would build up rapport with my clients so I could show up late or during lunchtime. When they replaced me they had to use two separate drivers. Even though I would get overtime every day, it was cheaper to pay it to me than to pay two other drivers each for eight-hour shifts.

Still, real estate is way different because I was so used to working on a schedule as a truck driver. Working real estate, I would go to bed at night and couldn't stop thinking about some of the escrows I had going on. I learned to write notes, leave myself messages on my desk so I wouldn't be afraid of forgetting something. It let me sleep better.

I had headaches for months in real estate because I wasn't used to using my brain. Driving a truck was all habit to me. I never had much education. I had never thought of myself as an intelligent guy. My dad worked the tar out of me as a kid. I was never afraid of hard work and was always as tenacious as all get out.

This whole experience in real estate sales was a step of faith. I was nervous about the idea of opening my own business, of becoming my own CEO. I was scared. But I had family members who backed me up. Since I was a kid my dad said I should get involved in sales. My wife was behind me. It was important to have family members who solidly believed in me because there were a lot of times I doubted myself. I wanted to quit. My wife and family members probably believed in me more than I believed in myself.

Real estate has been a very prosperous profession for me. I've really been blessed. My prospects are good. And they keep on growing every year. I think it's the result of where the market is heading. I got started at a great time when the market was very good.

I've seen enough agents come and go. I can sometimes pick out the ones who will make it and the ones who won't, although sometimes people surprise me because they don't let their true colors show at first. Mike can tell. He has a real good eye for those he thinks will make it.

He saw it in me. It's a good thing, too, because I didn't see it in myself.

~

JILL SCHMIDT PARKS
'Anybody can be average'

(Jill Schmidt Parks grew up in the business at PMZ with her father, Phil Schmidt, one of the highest-performing agents in the country. See more from her in Chapters Three and Nine.)

Now working out of PMZ's Orangeburg Avenue office in Modesto, I was born in Modesto in 1979, to a father who is very business-oriented with high expectations. I learned from him how to pass those expectations along to my clients. Growing up as a little girl, it was always a fun thing to do to go to the office with my dad on Saturday mornings. He was always there seven days a week whether he needed to be or not, and was the one to turn off the alarm.

I don't know if I told him this, but the reason I went to college (at UC Santa Barbara, majoring in business economics and minoring in sports management) was that the whole family was very athletic. It was academics and sports. My parents liked to keep us busy; there was no time to get into trouble. If you chose not to play a sport, you got a job. Basically, sports were our jobs. As long as we earned good grades, did our sports and stayed on track, they'd cover everything else for us.

High school was at Davis High School in Modesto, where I graduated in 1997. Of course, I did sports in school: swimming and playing water polo. I didn't really know what I wanted to do in high school. In college, I loved business. It's the fact that it lets you control your own destiny. But I really liked the sports aspect of business and thought about getting into sports marketing.

At UCSB, where I did my minor in sports management, I filled out a proficiency form, questioning you about likes and dislikes and telling you about what careers in life are best for you. Number one for me came up as being a Realtor®. I said to myself, "You've got to be kidding. I cannot tell my dad." But he always taught us to follow our hearts and do what we like, just to stay on track no matter what we would choose.

In high school I started getting the car washed and the gas tank filled up for my dad. During summers I'd help my dad during the day. I'd schedule pest control work, do some filing and follow up on escrows with title companies. I'd help him out during summers in college too.

I told my father that I have no problem working, but I'm going to go out into the world and see what it's like. "If you want to come work for me, you can," he would tell me.

Still, I said, "I'm going out into the real world and getting my feet wet."

"In-between," he replied, "why don't you help me?" The market was booming and I always had a passion for real estate, but felt if I didn't take these other jobs before embarking on a real estate career, I wouldn't appreciate it as much as I otherwise would. And, I thought, if you don't experience new things, you won't find out what you really like. Plus, I didn't want to be one of those people who end up hating going to work every day but doing it for 40 years. I wanted to do something I loved. Anyway, I knew real estate would always be there.

Just out of college in 2001, I moved back to Modesto because it was so affordable. I put my resume out there, got a call from a recruiter and worked for Enterprise car sales. It was not satisfying. Meantime, my dad said," Just come and help me out as my assistant a little bit and learn the ropes. You can see if you like it while you continue looking for another job." I got my real estate license in 2002.

I wasn't married. I didn't have a family of my own. And the market was thriving.

I love my dad to death. He has several assistants. And I think there's something about working with family that can be difficult. But PMZ is a family-based company, a nice niche. We can have good or bad days at the office. We can't control every aspect of what our clients want. But at the end of the day, you want to go home to dinner and, now that I'm married, my dad will pick up my girls for me. It's nice.

Everything I know is because of him. I started out in 2002, going out with my dad on every listing appointment, meeting the clients. It was an amazing exercise. He is so amazing with people. I feel like sometimes when I'm talking with clients, I'm almost in his chair while he's talking with them. There is such a wealth of knowledge there, plus he's such a people person. I'm a quick learner. Besides, I thought there couldn't be a long learning curve with him; there wasn't time for that. It was like, I'd tell him, "Tell me, tell me once and I'll figure it out."

Nevertheless, I spent at least two years with him. It's almost like I shadowed him for a while. We were always together. It was like a continuing education for my future. I wouldn't have stuck around if I hadn't loved what I was doing. I can honestly say I loved it. And I was learning.

Now I do it all by myself. We both don't need to go out on listing appointments. If I get a call, I go out by myself.

Now that I'm married with two children, my husband sometimes questions why I do what I do. I think he would rather have a little more time at home with me instead of being married to a working mom with two kids. When I graduated from UC, I decided I'm only going to do a job I love. I didn't care if it took me 15 or 20 jobs to find the right one. It took me only two.

After two years spent with my dad, it was sink or swim. He'd stand by me when I was talking with clients or speaking with them on the phone. He would whisper, "Good job, good job." Sometimes I would say, "Leave me alone." I'd shoo him away. I'd tell him, "How do you think I've made it this far?" I acquired a comfort level. Now we share quite a large office together.

My dad has been doing real estate since 1974. All of our clients are very loyal. We get a lot of repeat and referral business. Our clients tell somebody else—a family member, colleague, friend or neighbor. It was great when the market was good. But right now, with prices and the market down to what it was when I first got into the business, we have a lot of my dad's clients' children who are becoming first-time homebuyers.

My dad does a lot of work with people from the Gallo Winery and the two hospitals in town. How we divide the clients up depends on whom they're recruiting. I work with young couples and families. We have a lot in common. So if it's a younger family with kids the age of my children or younger—or children in general—I'm more knowledgeable about the local schools, what there is to do and even the city's night life. My dad and I will take our clients on community tours. I take over with the younger families.

Many of them are moving from out of town; most rent at first. I get that instant bond or connection. Even the Gallo Winery does college recruiting. So I go on the bus tours with my dad. Modesto is a great place, but you have to know how to sell it to the right crowd—and the right generation. My dad and I balance each other out. He doesn't know the places college grads want to go, or where to head out on Friday nights or weekends.

With a down market, right now we're also doing a lot of short sales. We don't do any bank-owned properties. We consistently stay busy enough with traditional buyers and sellers, and we don't want to take away from that.

But no matter the market, I'm not going anywhere. I know my dad isn't going anywhere. We're going to be doing this for many years. I'm in it for the long haul. Anybody can be average. In my family, we weren't raised that way. You do it and you give it 100 percent. There isn't any other way. It's all or none.

The nice thing about working with my dad is, although rarely is there a time when someone isn't here to cover the business, about once a year we do leave town at the same time, just the two of us. We're both very controlling people and we like to know something is getting done right. It's not like you're passing off a job for someone else to do and hoping it gets done. We tried that. It's an accountability thing. If I make a phone call to ask somebody else to make a phone call, I just as well should make the call myself. We count on each other and are content to know one of us is nearly always here.

The bottom line is simple: Work hard now and play later—and like it. People who aren't happy with what they do are not going to make people happy when they're doing it. You have to get up in the morning and like who you are and what you do. You can't do a job unless you like it.

I had never seen a down market before. My dad had, but he says he's never seen one this challenging. I look for tomorrow and say, "Let's just get through it and stay positive." We're surviving, including financially because we didn't blow through everything we earned in past years when the market was good. When the market was good, we knew it wouldn't last forever, and we were prepared for when it went down. We could have spent everything. We still put money in our retirement accounts, pay our taxes and put extra money away.

Chapter Two

Working Hard

During the 1980s, PMZ had a highly successful campaign featuring large outdoor billboards. It was inspired by something my father, Paul M. Zagaris, who founded PMZ, told me, which was the only thing that sells real estate is shoe leather. So the billboards depicted a giant photo of the sole of a shoe, above which were the following words: "Our shoe leather sells your real estate."

No matter how many tools, technologies or techniques may be available to real estate agents, at the end of the day, every successful agent is somebody who understands the importance of working hard. I've noticed in the last few years as the market changed so dramatically, those who always understand the importance of working hard and are willing to adapt to a changing environment continue to prosper.

At the end of the day there is just no substitute for hard work.

There are people who have gone into real estate, fewer in recent years, coming into the profession and thinking this is an easy way to make a good living. They're wrong. It's a great way to make a good living, but it's certainly not easy and it never will be.

My mission is to create the best possible environment I possibly can for individuals who are self-starting and hard-working people. No brokerage firm will ever make a successful real estate agent. Successful real estate firms can only create positive environments where people who are willing to work hard and smart can thrive.

I'm proud to be associated with so many fine real estate

professionals on our team who understand these realities. Samples of their stories are highlighted in this chapter.

~

DONALD & DORA OLIVERIA
'Just working hard'
'Anybody can be average'
(Both Donald and Dora are disciplined, high performing agents.)

Donald: I was born in Newmarket, Canada, near Toronto, in 1964. My dad was a truck driver. My mom worked as a seamstress in a factory. My parents moved back and forth from Portugal, spending about an equal amount of time in each country. I graduated high school in Canada and did all kinds of work: landscaping, construction, cleaning buildings and maintenance.

After high school, I moved back to Portugal, driving a truck and doing construction work for eight years. I met my wife, Dora, in Portugal. We married and she immigrated to the U.S. in 1990, to Santa Clara, California, where Dora was raised and knew the area.

Dora: I was born in Portugal in 1970. My parents immigrated to the U.S. in 1975, when I was five years old, to where they had family in the Central Valley. Two years later, in 1977, we moved to Santa Clara. My dad was in construction, doing dry wall. My mom stayed home to work.

After graduating from high school in Santa Clara in 1987, I moved back to Portugal with my parents, who by then were semi-retired because they had invested in California real estate. I met Donald in Portugal in '87, when he moved from Canada the same year. We were married in 1989.

When we moved to Santa Clara in 1990, we came with $1,700 in our pockets. Donald did construction, dry-wall for housing.

Donald started his own landscaping business in 1992. We moved to Turlock and he commuted for four years. He'd leave before dawn and come back after dusk. The money from his business was pretty good, but it was not a very good quality of life.

Donald and I started becoming interested in real estate. In 1995 we bought a house in Turlock. Reasonable home prices brought us to the Central Valley. We had our first child and figured Turlock, as a smaller community, was a better area to start a family. My family owned dairies, too.

I worked as a receptionist for a real estate broker, my first employer. I found a job in Hughson, selling bovine genetics and doing international marketing for 10 years. I figured you do what you want to do and get where you want to get.

Donald was slowly switching his landscape business from the San Francisco Bay Area to the Central Valley so that he was comfortable selling the landscape business in the Bay Area. He worked in the valley for a year or two and then got his real estate license. He sold the landscape business and went full throttle into real estate in 2000.

Donald: What attracted me to real estate from the landscape business was I wanted to get out of the heat and cold. I knew some people in real estate, and that's how I got into it.

I did real estate by myself until 2005. Then Dora's company was bought out and moved its headquarters to Canada. She studied for her real estate license and decided to help me part time. That worked out well. It turned into a full-time-plus job for her.

Both of us came from immigrant backgrounds.

Dora: We both saw our parents do what they had to do to get where they were. They were real traditional and goal oriented. They didn't believe in credit cards for years and years. If you needed something, you had to have the money to buy it. If you didn't have the money, you didn't buy it.

We learned from them how to save and how to work hard. Both our parents were very successful immigrants. We saw them work very hard. That helped. Our parents gave us that discipline.

Donald: I get along with people. I talk with everybody I see; I don't care who they are. We often end up talking about real estate, especially at that time when I started out and most Realtors® had their badges displayed on their shirts. People would see a Realtor® and talk about how the market is. Of course, you go to the people you know, those within your sphere of influence, and talk with them. You get yourself out there. I talked with a lot of people.

I did a lot of floor time in the office. I knocked on doors. When I was doing both jobs, I handed out real estate business cards to some of my landscape clients. I didn't get deals from them, but I did get deals from people I met through them.

It's just the process of seeing and talking with people—of going to functions, meeting people here and there. There are a lot of people out there who want to buy and sell. You just have to meet them.

At that time, you had to do your presentation and convince people you were good for the job, that you could list and sell their properties. I think I'm very good at it. I'm a good listener. If you had listings then, you had paychecks.

When Dora started working with me, things changed a lot. We built up a good referral database—people who were happy with our work. They told friends and relatives. That's where a lot of our business came from. Dora coming in made it even better. I could spend more time out there when she could take care of things at the office. And we're both good with people.

Dora: I started doing marketing. That allowed Donald to go out and be face-to-face with past clients. He'd show up, do "pop-byes" and reconnect on a regular basis.

We set annual goals. At the end of each year we'd review the past year. We'd look at spreadsheets showing total transactions and of them, what percentage was from buyers, repeat clients, referrals and listings. We tried to keep it balanced so we were prepared for any changes in the market.

We made adjustments. Every year we bumped it up, trying to do better each time. At the end of each quarter, we'd see where we were at, what our numbers were and how close we were to meeting our goals in terms of the number of transactions for the year.

We just figured that we had to work harder. That's how we planned our vacations. If we were behind where we thought we should be, we just kicked it up another notch and worked harder.

Donald: And we do push each other. We're always working harder. We're where we need to be most of the time. It's not easy to work harder when we spend 12 to 16 hours together working, either at the office or doing visits. We rarely have 8-hour days. There are some very long days.

Weekends, we try to dedicate to family. Saturdays we work, obviously. But Sunday is definitely a family day. We have two daughters who both play traveling sports. We don't miss games.

Obviously, the down market is difficult to predict; 2006-2007 were tough years for everybody, but we tried to set higher goals every year anyway even as we switched from a regular market to declining prices and foreclosures.

We keep a balance on types of transactions. We were pretty balanced between listings and buyers in the previous market. Lately, I've definitely done more with listings of bank-owned properties and foreclosed homes because that's where the market is. A lot of clients are banks or lenders.

We still have a clientele of investors, people who buy properties. We do a lot of work with them.

We want to be with both because there will come a time when the REO (real estate owned) market will stop. Then you will still need that traditional buyer clientele. You'll be a dead fish in the water if you don't have other people to work with.

Dora: We're trying to prepare to function in both markets. We continue to build our database. We use our buyer information from the REOs and add them to our database.

Donald: The first step in any transaction you have is making sure the clients are happy. You inform them of everything that is involved with escrow; we keep them well informed about everything going on with their transactions. A happy client will tell his or her friends and family members. A happy client can tell 100 other people.

We have a lot of repeat clients. They say we as a team provide a good service. When clients try to reach us we always answer them promptly. If something is going wrong with a transaction, we let them know so they are informed. And we fix it when it goes wrong.

Dora: We do have a licensed full time assistant handling transactions once they're in escrow, doing the coordination and a lot of the paperwork, especially with REOs. That allows us to be out more on the outside.

We both like to do what we do. We both enjoy our jobs and our profession. We foresee continuing and making necessary adjustments as the market changes. Real estate is constantly changing. We attend seminars, educate ourselves and get prepared for whatever comes our way. Seminars help us see what's coming so we know what we need to do to adjust.

Donald: We try to be well informed with what's going on in the market, whichever market it is.

Dora: We also love PMZ, where we've been since 2005. We both went to PMZ shortly after I joined the business. We could see the market was going to change and PMZ was definitely ahead of the curve in technology. We felt it was definitely the right time and the right move.

Donald: I always felt PMZ is a step ahead in technology compared to other real estate companies. I remember being at another company where my clients would tell me they were looking for properties on the PMZ website. It's easy to use and super user-friendly with lots of listings.

~

MEREDITH BRANDSMA
'Disciplined about keeping to the schedule'
*(She's built success around working directly with
people. See more in Chapters Three and Six.)*

I'm not a believer that by sitting at home or doing floor time twice a week or by doing open houses every weekend—that those things in and of themselves are going to create business.

But I did do all of those things. I feel most confident and most engaged when I am one-on-one with people. Open houses did work very well. I was able to get quite a few clients just because I did two open houses every weekend and engaged people in conversation, discovered what they were looking for, followed up with them afterwards and worked those angles. That was where my comfort level was.

It wasn't doing cold calls. They were a bit of a struggle. In some of our classes and seminars you're really encouraged to go down that road. By not following that path I felt maybe I wasn't doing the right thing. But that wouldn't have been the right thing for me. What I did was the right thing for me. I knew I was good with people. I knew that was where a lot of my energy comes from. I'm a pretty big extrovert. I do need my down or alone time, but I'm a team player. I like to have people to bounce ideas off of and to share things with. That's when I feel I'm doing my best work and the most good on behalf of my career.

In the beginning, when I first got started, my schedule was definitely structured around what my background had been in the non-profit corporate world where I had worked for years. I was in the office every day by 8 a.m. I sat at my desk until 12 noon. I found work to do for myself. I did things because I was there. I'd buzz out of the office for an hour and a half to recharge, come home, get some lunch and go back to the office or go out, as one of my Realtor®

mentors said, to do "belly to belly visits." That's getting in front of people belly-to-belly and talking with them face to face. These were typically not cold calls. I was going to people I knew and dropping in to say hello, hand out some of my business cards and ask if they knew anybody interested in buying or selling property. That was where I felt most at home and it's what produced business for me.

It hasn't changed that significantly since then. I'm busier now so my days are structured a little differently. I'm still always in the office between 8 and 8:30 a.m. I do all of my calls and paperwork—most of my deskwork—in the morning hours because that's when I feel sharpest, on top of things. It's when I feel the energy starting to go down that I schedule people-to-people meetings in the afternoons. I just know when I'm with people I get my energy from them. They energize me. That also works out the best anyway since most of my clients work and have to get together with me in the afternoon or evening hours.

I'm still very disciplined about scheduling myself and keeping to the schedule.

~

WAYNE JONES
'Persistence is the key to success'
(Now a very successful real estate agent, Wayne learned how to overcome difficulties through tenacity.)

By the time I was born in 1945, my dad was finished working in shipyards down in the Long Beach area. Then he held some odd jobs—truck driving and manual labor—after which he didn't work for a number of years. My mom was an administrative person, a secretary to presidents of corporations, for as long as I could remember.

I was brought up in Southern California, going to L.A. city schools and graduating from high school in the San Fernando Valley.

Then it was back to attend Long Beach City College. Growing up, I wanted to be a dentist but thought better of it after taking chemistry classes. I didn't buckle down and have the drive to focus because I was more involved in earning a living, having married fairly young and being saddled with responsibilities.

Although I left home under adverse circumstances, feeling I was suffering under a domineering father, I didn't realize at the time it was a loving home. So I started out with menial jobs. The first one as a teenager lasted four days, standing up all day long turning rubber gloves inside out one by one. I worked at a valve company for six months and applied to Douglass Aircraft in Long Beach for a pilot training program. I did well with them, was taught to read blueprints and how to do quality assurance. I worked myself up over a period of five or six years into a pretty good position with the company and had a number of people under me. However, after a number of years at Douglass, I watched as they were laying off men in other areas of the company who were there way longer than me and approaching retirement age. I didn't understand why they were keeping me, a punk kid.

Meantime, I heard about the outside sales field, which interested me. So I landed a job selling for the Yellow Pages, and I've been in sales ever since.

While still at Douglass, I was of draft age and it was during the Vietnam War. Word came I would be drafted. I passed the physical and thought the next step would be receiving a draft notice. So I joined the National Guard, a six-year obligation. I had just gotten married and had two children in quick succession. So I was working at Douglass and did the National Guard one weekend a month.

I found out in the Guard there was a way to become a commissioned officer by attending Officer Candidate School. At the time, the California National Guard had an O.C.S. program on weekends. I received training on leadership and was commissioned as an officer.

During the first three of my six years of National Guard service, I pretty much goofed off. But after a year in O.C.S., I settled down and really enjoyed the training and leadership skills, seeing how they also helped me through life, giving me the skills to teach and influence others.

I also gravitated into real estate when I was younger, in the 1970s. I started out and did pretty well as an individual investor, buying and selling real estate. I bought my first house for $18,500, in Long Beach, a little two-bedroom, one-bath. It was a struggle to put together the $1,850 down payment. Part of it was put on a credit card. I financed the other 10 percent of the down payment with a second deed of trust.

Then, two years later we moved to Orange County, where I bought a house in Garden Grove, paying $29,000. Then a couple of years later I bought another house, 2,000 square feet and also in Garden Grove, for $54,000.

With these successes in real estate, my ego was growing pretty big. I saw another, bigger house in the subdivision. I kept my house and bought another. Soon there were opportunities to buy a duplex and four-plex. I bought a couple of rental houses during the same time frame.

I was doing pretty well. I remember my pastor telling me, "You'll either make it big or lose it all." It turned out he was correct. I wound up pretty much losing it all and getting down to ground zero financially. But my interest in real estate had been piqued.

After the Yellow Pages job, I wound up selling office products—copy machines—and moved up to Northern California, living with my folks in the Bay Area during the early '80s, after the divorce. It was start-over time. After two years with the folks, I moved back to Orange County, working there selling copy machines too. I couldn't bring myself to buy real estate in the same places where I had previously owned.

I bought a house in Modesto in the late '80s, my first house there. I had a reputable agent who would show me properties while driving us in his expensive car. Three times, I expressed an interest in a house because the exterior appealed to me. He heard me but didn't listen to what I said. He proceeded to show another house he was interested in selling me. After the third time of him not showing me the house I was interested in, I called another agent. She showed me the home at 4:30 on a Saturday. We met the next morning, wrote up an offer and I bought that house.

It sat vacant. On weekends, I brought in furniture. But I was still selling office copiers and needed to make the break from Southern California to Modesto. Finally, I got my real estate license in 1989, and was encouraged to quit my copier job and go into real estate full time. That I did.

Persistence is the key to success. You have to persevere if you want to succeed at anything. I am the kind of person who likes to succeed. If I endeavor to do anything, I want to excel at it. I tried doing that over the years. Any position I have held, I've tried to achieve a measure of success. I did that selling office machines, copiers. I also struggled and struggled in real estate.

I was not as well connected as some, not as social and outgoing as some. So I worked very hard at it, stayed at the job and persisted through difficult times. I kept my lifestyle down so I was living within my means. But I can't say the actual turnabout came about from my doing. You're just blessed. I had a relationship with a broker who was grounded in Christian principles. He gave me referrals and I paid him fees. That's part of how real estate works.

When I lost my house in 1992 in Modesto, through a short sale to a struggling market and a struggling income, I needed a place to move. One of my listings was for a condo. The owner wanted to get rid of it. He sold it to me in exchange for taking over the existing loan and for an $8,000 note back to him as a second that was my down payment. I didn't know where I was going to live after walking away from my house. I had no money. I was selling real estate, but struggling.

The good news was it was a good place to live, and I got all of this built-in business. There were 34 units in that complex, called the Newporter. I got to sell a minimum of 13 of them in the following two years. That helped kick start my business. Things picked up from there.

I attribute my turnaround to perseverance despite adversity. They are the only words that make a lot of sense. Even though you have difficult times, you keep going. A negative situation turned into a positive one for me.

The last few years have been the best I've had in my real estate career—during the toughest market I've seen. I've worked really hard. It's not uncommon for me to put in a 12-hour day during busy times. But it produces results.

You have to stay focused on what you're doing. When I'm at work, I'm at work; I stay focused on my work. I keep my focus on the tasks at hand. In doing that, sometimes your peers misread you and you are perceived as being anti-social. They think you're ignoring them. My colleague Tim Rhode is almost apologetic to his peers if he thinks he offends anyone. But I don't take time to commiserate with misery.

That little condo I bought? I eventually sold it and was able to put $60,000 down on the house I live in today in the College area of Modesto, a good location. Over the past few years, when my business took off, I was able to do $70,000 worth of improvements, paid for with cash. Then, in early 2009, I was able to retire the mortgage. I acquired another property in Modesto and retired the mortgage on it too. I own it clear now.

~

MIKE BAZUIK
'If you're willing to work, real estate is a great field to be in'
(Practicing with his wife, Roxanne, Mike has built a career on discipline and hard work. See more from Mike in Chapters Six, Nine and Eleven.)

I was born in Castro Valley in 1960; my father had a stainless steel fabrication shop building equipment for hospitals, jails and restaurants. My mother was a real estate agent, accountant and bookkeeper. She started real estate on the side as a second career when my folks split up.

I grew up in Hayward, lived in Fremont for a good time and then moved to Modesto at the age of 20. Afterwards, we moved back and forth from Modesto to Manteca. I went to Laney College and did the apprenticeship program in sheet metal. I worked for my dad's shop, ran his business after he had some strokes, and went to work for a competitor before starting my own stainless fabrication shop and running it for about 10 years. We were commuting to Union City, where we were renting. I bought a 10,000 square foot building in Manteca and ran the business out of there. I was about 40 when I got into real estate. My mom originally got me into real estate. When I was 18, we partnered in buying a condo in Newark.

I had about seven rentals in the East Bay and the Modesto area that I was managing. We had just bought a house in Modesto.

As I was trying to get out of the stainless steel business, I got a contractor's license and started to become a building inspector. But it was in the middle of a downturn and no one was hiring. I asked myself, "What the heck do I do?" I had those seven rental properties, and liked them. I had dealt with several Realtors® in buying those properties. I thought, "I could do a better job than they did." So I obtained my license. It wasn't that hard to get.

If you're willing to put the time in and work the business, real estate is a great field to be in. You meet a lot of nice people out there.

The income can be just phenomenal if you're willing to put in the time.

I was fortunate. I talked with Mr. Zagaris and he said he wanted to send me to a seminar teaching agents how to be agents. They were teaching prospecting: What do you say when you prospect? How do you handle questions during presentations? I thought this was so cool.

I started role-playing five days a week, as soon as I got in to work in the morning, usually around 6:30 or 7. We'd say affirmations to ourselves for a minute. (When I turned my cell phone on in the morning, it usually popped up with my name and phone number. I deleted that and instead put in: "I'm good. I'm great. I'm powerful." Those are affirmations I like to use to start the day.

Then I'd get into the role-playing as part of the program for 10 minutes. Next I was calling listings that were for sale by the owners, or they were expired or withdrawn because the clients didn't like the agents, or the listings expired because the house didn't sell. Every morning I'd sit down for two and a half hours, shut the door and do what I called "dialing for dollars."

I was on a very disciplined prospecting routine. The difference between me and most other agents was, for nine years I came in at 6:30 a.m. and prospected from 7:30 until 11. The only other people who showed up at 8 a.m. were those who were paid on the book. Most agents didn't show up until 9 or 10 a.m. "Holy smokes, how do they make a living?" I asked myself.

A lot of people are up early. Sometimes, I'd door knock starting at 7:45 a.m. I could cover almost 300 homes in the morning. Most people weren't there, so I'd leave something on the door. Most people weren't mean or nasty. They'd open up the door and say, "Hi." Even today, I'll call people up: "Hi, I'm Mike Bazuik, and I'm in real estate. I just listed a house down the block or on whatever street. It's a two-bedroom, two-bath, 1,500 square foot house for $130,000. Who do you know who wants to move into this nice area?" Some have friends or relatives. If they say no, I ask if they ever thought of real estate as a way to supplement their income or retirement. If they're interested, I explain we're in one of the best times to buy real estate. If they say no, I ask if they have any other real estate needs. If they say no, I thank them and hang up.

Now I'm working on trying to find short sales, people who need to get out of their houses. The list of homes in Manteca that are in pre-foreclosure goes to 300. I tried driving by those addresses and leaving door hangers. It wasn't that successful. I need to talk to them, not leave anything. So I get the phone numbers so I can call them up.

In one recent year I sold nine bank-owned properties, REOs (real estate owned). Before that I was doing BPOs, broker price options. I still do them. Banks would send me a list with homeowners who were pulling money out of their houses' equity. The banks asked me to obtain three comps, three active listings and three recently sold properties. Then they asked me to take front and side pictures of the houses and upload all of that so they could determine if they wanted to lend the money.

After I finished prospecting every day at around 11 a.m., I'd go out and start doing my BPOs. In the afternoons, I'd make appointments with people I had spoken with on the phone in the morning to do presentations. Or I'd get ready for presentations to buyers or sellers that I set up in the evening hours.

I still look for consumers trying to sell. They may provide me with a daughter, friend or work colleague who may want to buy a house. I still follow up and work with buyers.

I apply the same discipline no matter how the market shifts. You just have to follow the market and see what direction it's going in and then try to jump onto the biggest portion of it.

The way it started out, in my first year in real estate, I worked six and a half days a week. In the second, third and fourth year, I was working six days a week. The other day I was on site (at the office) at 6 a.m. and walked in the door of my house at 7 p.m.—so that was a

13-hour day. On another day I will probably get in at 6:50 a.m. and will probably get home around 6 p.m.—for 11 hours. But I'm taking off tomorrow to go golfing and I'm not working on Sunday.

The time I take on or off goes with the market. As we were rolling in 1996, '97 and '98, I was golfing every Friday. The banks were loading me up with deals. I was busy four days a week but took off every Friday and most Saturdays. When the market changed, I was back to buying and fixing up properties, doing the physical labor, installing cabinets in homes and then flipping them.

We finished one house I bought for $139,500. We sanded and re-stained all the cabinets, painted the interior with two-tone paint. We put in all new light fixtures and doors, all new linoleum throughout, all new carpeting and padding. I put about $7,500 into that one. We sold it for $189,000. Another gentleman who helped me and I did all the work. I probably spent two weeks over there doing the labor.

~

ROSA GONZALEZ
'You have to work hard'

(She learned the business from the ground up. For more on Rosa, see Chapters Three, Six and Nine.)

I have some simple advice: Treat your business like a business. Know you are the CEO of your company. Then you have to work hard. Mike Zagaris tells us one of the big gifts his parents gave him—his father was a coal miner—was the knowledge that you had to work hard. My parents instilled that in me as well. There is true beauty in that because it makes you a good person. You feel good about yourself.

I'm one of 15 children. The achievements my parents earned were through hard work.

I believe there is so much respect and knowledge in valuing hard work. I think people too often want to earn money the easy way. I see so many people in this industry who really don't want to put in the hours. But you just have to. There's a beauty in it.

Chapter Three

Taking Care of Your Clients

Being successful in real estate is made far easier when you recognize the importance of developing business from a base of people you know and providing those with whom you work with the highest level of service.

Too many agents and too many real estate industry gurus focus on developing business by cold calling, which is typified by unsolicited telephone calls directed to people the agents don't know. This type of business development does not usually generate a high rate of return.

The reason is simple: The people agents are calling don't know them. No rapport has been established. Yet many real estate sales authorities lead agents down this path.

Most real estate offices feature opportunity time. An agent who is on opportunity time spends hours waiting for calls coming into the office from prospective clients who are not assigned to a specific agent. There is no question business can develop this way. But it is not and should never be a primary source of business. It's analogous to sitting in a boat waiting for the fish to jump out of the water and into your lap. Sometimes it happens that way, but you can't build a career on it. This is not a proactive, agent-driven pursuit. Like other passive types of business endeavor, it is not central to creation of a good practice. Those who rely on such strategies typically fail to succeed in our field.

By concentrating on strategies such as cold calling, agents fail to pay adequate attention to the importance of taking care of clients once they are working with them. The top-performing agents tend to be men and women who understand the importance of working with people they know as well as those who are referred to them by the people they know. The robust nature of a successful practice grows directly in relation to the quality of service agents provide their clients.

What agents should constantly be striving for in a client-centered practice is the combination of providing outstanding service to those with whom they are working, coupled with a business development strategy centered on seeking referrals from people who have been well served. That is the cornerstone of a great agent's business.

From a business development perspective, it is far more valuable to center on communicating with people you know, people who know people you know or people for whom you have a potentially valuable message to impart. For example, existing residents in a neighborhood where you have listed a home are often very interested in receiving information about that home. Going door to door to speak with them can lead to dialogue and perhaps establishment of a relationship.

It isn't very productive to call people out of the blue with no useful information, relying on a script and pitch that may not be related to their lives. The best way to prospect is to talk with people you know or have done business with in the past or those for whom you have genuinely valuable information.

I experience this phenomenon as a broker every day I'm developing business by recruiting real estate professionals. People in the business I already know frequently refer them. If I do a good job of taking care of the agents who work with PMZ, they talk well of me.

But here's the catch that many in our field miss: If I fail to ask these people who have a good opinion of me for their help—if I don't let them know I'm interested in their assistance in identifying others who may want to work with me—they may appreciate me, but they may not provide the referrals I seek.

So there are two things I need to do: Take care of the agents who work with me so they're happy and productive. And I need to ask these agents and others I meet for their help in getting me further business.

Agents face the same requirements. First, they need to take good care of their clients. When that happens the grateful clients will say, "Thank you very much. I can't thank you enough." The agents should then reply, "I value your thoughts and would appreciate it if you would do something for me: If you hear of anyone interested in buying or selling a home, let me know." Most of them will.

A great place to start for those just coming into the business is their friends, relatives, neighbors—anyone they know. They don't have to directly ask for business. They only have to ask for assistance—if these friends or relatives would be willing to give some support by providing contacts with people who may be interested in buying and selling.

You don't have to ask, "Hey, Fred, will you use me when you need a real estate agent?" Instead, you say, "Fred, I've set some big goals for myself. And I know with your help and the help of friends like you I can attain my goals. I'd appreciate it if you'd do me a favor."

"What is it?" Fred will ask.

"If you know anyone interested in buying or selling real estate, would you please let me know?" you respond.

Invariably, Fred will say, "Sure."

You follow up that conversation with a communication, a hand-written or printed card, thanking Fred for his support.

Agents who want to expand their practice more rapidly can make a list of everyone they know in the community being targeted—friends, relatives or acquaintances. Then they put the list—and additional contacts that are made—into a database and systematically start contacting all of them.

Every one of us has a pair of eyes. Successful agents recruit scores and scores of individuals in the community to be on the lookout for leads they can refer to their friend in the real estate business. Creating this army of friends and relatives who act on the agent's behalf is part of how a great real estate practice is created.

The best agents spend most of their time on the care and feeding of their referral base and sphere of influence— the people they know through community involvement plus past clients, friends and relatives. It is proper and regular communication with this database and sphere of influence that builds the foundation for the growth of their practices.

Additionally, any time leads are generated from the database, it is important to call or send a note to those who referred you and thank them—let them know how meaningful it is for your success.

The next imperative in a client-centered practice is once you start working with clients, provide them with the best and most responsive professional service. It's only by providing great service that agents win loyal allies for the rest of their careers. It is by taking care of people that agents ensure people will take care of them.

The most successful agents I know have hundreds of clients they have served well. These clients feel good about the job the agent did for them and are confident the agent will do a similar job for anyone they refer. It is important for the agent to stay in regular communication with former clients, asking for their ongoing help through referrals.

The most successful real estate agents weave themselves into the fabric of the communities in which they live and serve. They are actively involved in charitable, community, religious, civic or political affairs. Many agents coach soccer and Little League. Because of this participation they come in daily contact with lots of people. That definitely increases the number of their acquaintances and it can dramatically expand their sphere of influence.

Agents take part in these activities because they are meaningful in and of themselves. You don't coach soccer for your kids or join a church just to get more business. But as a result of giving selflessly of your energy and time, you come to know many like-minded people who come to know and trust you—and ultimately, when the time is right, do business with you or refer business to you.

There is another key element to a client-centered practice that is often overlooked: the nature of the relationship between agents and their clients.

Agents are getting paid to provide a service. Therefore, they have an obligation to be sensitive about how their clients think and communicate.

Ever meet someone with whom you have an instant rapport—someone with whom you instantly feel at ease? It can be a person who coincidentally shares your mannerisms. Or it could be someone who is so perceptive that they adapt their own communication style with your own to strike an immediate bond. Such people have mastered the internal technology of analyzing human communication and applying it in their relations with others.

People think and communicate in different ways. They have different ways of relating to the world. Agents have a duty to modify their way of communicating to accommodate the communication style of their clients. This process is called building rapport.

In relationships between friends or spouses there is an equal obligation on the part of both parties to meet one another at a central or neutral place. When two human beings are involved in friendships or marriages, no one is getting paid.

But agents are getting paid to be real estate professionals. It is a fundamentally different kind of relationship. Agents can't expect their clients to change their way of communicating.

Some people speak in visual terms. They say things like, "I can see what you're talking about." When they speak of a home, they comment on what they see, offering visual clues.

Others talk about how they feel; they respond in sensory terms. Such people may say, "I really felt warm when I walked into that home."

Still others respond in auditory terms: "I hear what you're saying."

The job of a real estate professional is to be sensitive to how people choose to communicate and then communicate with them in a manner closely approximating that form.

If their goal is achieving a client-centered practice by taking care of their clients, agents have to go where their clients are. Agents can't expect their clients to come to them.

Any number of agents who work with me have provided valuable insights on these topics. Here are but a few of their stories.

❧

PAM HARMON
'Treating Clients Like Family'

(I have come to respect Pam Harmon, a native of Modesto with a real knack for the real estate business, as a genuine professional.)

I was born in Modesto in 1952, the youngest of three children. My father was a farmer. My grandfather was a farmer. I come from a great, Christian-centered family. I grew up loving the land.

My parents taught me very young the importance of integrity and standing behind what you say. My father taught me how to shake hands using a firm grip. "When you shake hands," he said, "that is giving your word. Never go back on it." He taught me that in past generations when people were selling something to someone for X number of dollars and they shook hands on it, it was like a written contract.

I always kept in my head that what I said and my actions affect what happens next. It could be for something happening right now or it could be for something occurring years from now.

I started selling at a young age. When I was 10, my father had me put together a report to present to the banker on how I would borrow money to buy some cattle. He took me to Crocker Bank downtown. "I'm going to stay in the lobby," he said. "You're prepared. You've done your homework. You show the banker how you're going to pay him back for the money you're going to borrow." I went into the meeting by myself. They loaned me the couple of thousand dollars to buy the cattle.

In the morning I had to go out and bottle-feed some of the calves. Some died on me. At a young age I realized I had a debt to pay; if they kept dying on me, what would I do next?

I was able to raise and sell the cattle and pay off the bank. That was my first venture in financing, in borrowing money and knowing about my asset and debt load.

The next year a farmer was raising watermelons across from our place, 20 miles outside Modesto. They were picking and loading melons on trailers. I went over, introduced myself and asked to set up a fruit stand to sell his watermelons there on Shiloh Road due west of town.

The farmer said I would never be able to sell way out there. "Would you please give me a shot?" I asked. He agreed to give me one trailer load. "You do the best you can," he said.

He ended up bringing me a trailer load of watermelons every day. I don't know where all those people came from. On weekends, people came from as far away as the Bay Area. I made him more money off my little fruit stand than he made from some of the grocery stores.

So I grew up loving both the land and working with people. After graduating from high school and taking classes at different colleges, I thought my major would be accounting because I loved numbers. But I always knew I loved to sell too.

During this time I married and put my career on the back burner while being a wife and mother. We now have two children, a son and daughter, and four grandchildren.

When the kids were junior high school age, I took the state exam for my real estate license, passed it and started working.

I just love my profession. I get the greatest joy out of helping people. My business is truly based on my clients. It goes back to handshaking. If you take care of them, they will be loyal to you. They will tell their family and friends about you.

I've had clients where it took me two years to help them clean up their credit and get them on a budget so they could qualify to buy a home. Sometimes I've talked people out of buying when that's what they wanted to do but I knew they couldn't afford it. Their family life was not together; they had so many financial problems that if the debt load from buying the house was added it would only cause their credit to go down or place more stress on their marriage. I'd keep telling them that even though they shouldn't buy a home right away, they needed to have that as their goal. I encouraged them to save and strive for it. "We're going to make it as a team," I would say.

I prefer the team approach. I work for my clients. They hire me. Sometimes that means helping them improve their financial situation so they can buy a house.

A single mother with two teenagers approached me, interested in buying a home, but she couldn't qualify. First, we met with a lender who analyzed what our situation was. (I always say our situation because I become so much a part of their lives. It's really personal for me.) The loan officer said my client needed to clean up some issues on her credit, pay off some debt and establish a record of paying bills in a timely fashion.

That's what she had to do for a while to establish her credit. So that's what we did. I put her on a budget. I held her accountable. I checked in on her every month to make sure the bills were being paid on time and she was saving X amount of money out of every paycheck.

We worked on it for two years. Meantime, we kept looking for houses so I could show her what was out there—to help her keep up on the market and to encourage her. She had to see the light at the end of the tunnel.

We found the cutest little house in northeast Modesto. It needed some paint and cleanup. But it had a solid structure. She qualified after two years. The joke we would tell was that I looked so long that if she didn't buy something soon she would have to get me a new set of tires.

When you wait and want something so bad and struggle and save for so long, you know what it means when you finally receive it? There is great satisfaction. My client is still in that house and doing very well.

I'm so fortunate to be on the sidelines and see that kind of joy and satisfaction. Some of my clients have become like family. They even come to Christmas dinner—like Craig and Michelle. They were from back east. He came out here to take a job as CEO at a local company. They were flying in and he asked if I could pick him and his family up and show them the town.

When clients come from out of the area, I try to educate them on the city and the area around it. Then, over time, whether it is one, two or three trips, I get to know them and have a good handle on their lifestyle and what they're looking for in a home.

I remember one couple to this day. He was reserved. They had adopted a little boy from Korea, Tyler, who was about one and a half or two years old. We looked for houses for a long time. Michelle, the wife, kept saying she needed to be close to the hospital. I found out she was a kidney transplant recipient, had continuing health problems and needed to always be within a certain number of miles of the hospital.

Craig, her husband, traveled on business all over the world. He would sometimes be gone overseas three weeks out of the month. They had no family here. I told Michelle, "Here's my cell and home phone numbers. If you ever need me, call no matter the time."

I'll never forget one Thursday morning when I was headed into the office for a meeting. The cell phone rang. It was Michelle. "Pam, I need to go to the hospital. Can you take me?"

My husband and I took her to the hospital so many times they thought my husband was her dad. They'd come out into the waiting room at 2 in the morning and say, "You can come in now and sit with your daughter."

She has a new kidney now and is doing well. Since then I've sold Craig, Michelle and their family several houses. They adopted a little girl from Korea. We were at the airport to help them pick her up.

Every other year we have a big barbecue in honor of Michelle's kidney. The last time there were 150 people over for dinner.

That's how I work. It's not for everybody in real estate. I look at this profession as my business. Even though I work with a company, PMZ, I'm independent. The business has to be based on who I am and how I want to take care of others.

That doesn't mean I can please everybody. I can't. I fail sometimes. But as long as I have a love of the profession, this is the only way I can do business.

Do you ever go visit someone in the hospital and meet a nurse who takes such good care of the patients? Then other times there can be a nurse who is tired or indifferent and doesn't treat people very well. I don't want to be like the indifferent nurse. When I lose the love of what I'm doing, it will be time for me to get out.

I started working in real estate in 1986, originally for a small mom-and-pop real estate company in Modesto when the market was flat during a recession. It was a good time to come into the business because that's when you learn. When things aren't very busy you have more time to learn how to do it right—to ask questions of other agents with experience who you respect. That's when you want to set your foundation in the profession.

I was selling about 10 homes a year at first. I learned a lot, but the small mom and pop office was difficult in some respects because it was very controlling and you couldn't expand. In the mid-1990s,

I was asked to join Re/Max, which was a giant step for me. I was there for nine months and sold substantially more. Back then, my commissions were around $65,000 a year. My goal for the following year was to make $100,000. Even though the market was still depressed, I met that goal the next year.

In January 2004 I came to PMZ. I didn't know Mike personally except to say hello, although I always knew about the company. They had a lot to offer in areas where I needed help for my clients.

Mike takes care of providing any tools we need to benefit our clients or ourselves. He is very bright, always striving and very goal oriented. I love to hear him talk. He is always educating and challenging us. This is an area where I feel as agents we really let ourselves down. It is so important to continue our education for our clients and ourselves.

At PMZ, I know I can improve and do more volume. Our market prices have gone up substantially, which means more in commissions. But I try not to place great emphasis on the number of transactions I do. It's charted, but if I only look at that, I would lose what I love about working.

I focus on customer service; client satisfaction is a better term. I don't look at the profession over just the next one to five years. I look at it as something I will do forever. My kids know I will probably never retire. When I'm gone, they will just put a "sold" sign over my casket.

I would like to take some more time off and do a few extra things. I can do that if I permit myself. I have that choice.

Now each year I do a little bit better. I want a gradual increase. A lot of times real estate has its peaks and valleys. But if you have a practice based on client satisfaction, you're more apt to have a slow, steady climb. It's like exercising on a treadmill: you increase the incline and speed over time and gradually get in better shape.

There is one area where I have come up short: Because all these years I did not have a database, I did not faithfully stay in contact with all of my clients. I kept in touch with many of them. But when it comes to hundreds of people, you lose track of some.

What's really interesting is now I am creating my own database with the computer support Mike gives me. I went back a number of years and entered old clients into it. Then I sent out a letter apologizing, saying it has been so long since I talked with them. The letter said I'm still around and I brought them up to date on my life. Emails came back from some of them saying they hadn't forgotten me.

I still get involved with my clients. It could be many months while I'm finding them a home or putting together financing. During that time I go to their weddings or their baby showers. I just got a call from the mom of a client; her daughter's baby was born yesterday. The other day my husband and I received an invitation from a past client to the ceremony for his son who is becoming an Eagle Scout.

That's the kind of joy I get from my work. What other profession gives you the opportunity to interact in the lives of such wonderful people?

The only negative aspect of the profession for me is you can't be close to all of them. You only have so much you can give. You get with them and talk to them regularly over many weeks. Then, once the transaction is finished, it's like a withdrawal. It's like when your child goes away to college and all of a sudden you have to cut the strings. That happens between client and real estate agent. You spend a lot of time together and become attached to each other.

~

MEREDITH BRANDSMA
'Listening carefully'
(Meredith also appears in Chapters Two and Six.)

Born in Michigan, I grew up there in a little town much like Modesto, a small rural community close to Grand Rapids. My dad was a detective with the Ottawa County Sheriff's Department. My interests went to performing—not that I was necessarily thinking of going into acting or entertainment. I just loved the arts, being on stage, an interest that really started as a junior high school student. I was involved in the choir and sang at church. It snowballed into a high school and college career.

My first two years as an undergraduate at Western Michigan University in Kalamazoo were spent as a vocal performance major concentrating on jazz music. Things changed between my junior and senior years. I saw lots of my peers who had much more talent and drive to make it a career than me. I switched over to arts administration, the business side of the performing arts world, and got a B.A. degree in arts administration in 1993.

Determined to get a job in the arts, for a year I worked three jobs or internships, two of them not paid, with arts organizations. Plus I waited tables. Then I got a break while performing with the Grand Rapids Symphony; I did children's concert performances. I was hired as the annual funds manager, in charge of fundraising development, and was with them for two years. At a certain point, I thought to myself, "I've done what I wanted to do here." You see, since high school I always wanted to move away, to try my hand in another city—not because I didn't have a great childhood or I didn't love my family. I just always wanted to become a big city gal.

Looking for another opportunity, I was hired as director of development for the Youth Orchestra in Minneapolis, Minnesota. Meantime, I also got married.

I was with the children's orchestra for about another two years, until 2004. My husband was offered a position in Modesto. He was brought out to be executive director of the Modesto Symphony Orchestra. Coming from a large metropolitan area to a smaller more agricultural community, I struggled to find something similar to the employment levels of my previous positions. The Gallo Center for the Performing Arts was not yet up and running at the time in

Modesto.

I looked for another job, did community volunteer work and supported my husband's efforts. Finally, I found something, once again in the fundraising field, for a foundation in town. It just wasn't the right fit. While at that job, I started exploring real estate. It always held an interest for me. I loved to go to open houses and see what was on the market. While exploring different aspects of real estate as a career, I realized all the things I loved most about my executive-level jobs really carried over into real estate.

Working in executive management, I loved the interaction between the employees I was overseeing and myself—trying to help them resolve their problems and crises, and making their jobs more interesting and rewarding. That's also what we ultimately try to do for our clients in real estate. We try to find the right fits for them as we help them navigate through the often-complicated real estate process. It's not always easy. Like my employees when I worked in the non-profit world, my real estate clients today don't always know how to vocalize what they need to make things easier and more efficient.

So you have to be very open and listen carefully in order to identify what they are really trying to say. I find that is definitely true in the home buying business with clients. They often enter the process thinking, "This is what I want." In reality, you have to ask the right questions to find out if that is actually the case.

Another cross-tie between the non-profit management world and practicing real estate is the negotiating end of it. In some real estate markets, there is a lot more negotiating that goes on. When I was in the non-profit world, we had to negotiate contracts, salaries and different arrangements with vendors. I always loved that part of it. There can be the same excitement in what goes on between listing agents, buyers and sellers.

I began in real estate in January 2006. I was fortunate. Moving to Modesto in 2004, we were introduced to broader and more varied segments of the community through the Modesto Symphony

Orchestra. Board members wanted to make sure we were quickly integrated into the community. We met many different people. I personally found Modesto an incredibly warm and gracious city. If you come in and express an interest in being a member of the community, you are really enveloped into it.

So I tapped into that group of people as best as I could. Of course, as many of them were already very established in the community, most already had Realtors® they liked working with. But enough were willing to pass my name around and put in a good word for me or actually use my services that it was a good place to start.

~

KAREN SERPA
'Staying in touch with people'
(See more about Karen, whose tenacity and integrity comes through here, in Chapters Six, Nine and Ten.)

I was born in Modesto in 1954; my dad was lots of things: a farm labor contractor, mechanic and car salesman. My mom was a stay-at-home mom and supported my dad most of the time. When I was 14, my dad had a heart attack and my mom went to work outside of the home for an international printing company in Modesto. She moved up the ladder until she was vice president of training, traveling all over the U.S. training people in management, sales and different other things.

I grew up in Hughson, a small town near Modesto, graduating from high school there in 1971. I wanted to be a teacher while I was growing up. As a horse lover, at one time I wanted to be a veterinarian. By the time high school graduation came, I had married my high school sweetheart and continued going to school. I earned an A.A. degree in business and accounting from the community college. I worked in banking for several years. I started filing checks and worked my way up to operations manager at a local bank branch in Fresno, where we moved in 1974.

After six or seven years in banking, I went to work in 1979 in the accounting department of a Coors beer distributor in Fresno doing their accounts receivable. My husband was sales manager for Napa Auto Parts distribution. I moved with him to Sacramento when he was transferred there in 1980.

When we left Hughson, I said I'd never go back. It's such a small town with nothing to do. Everyone knows everyone else's business. In 1982, we bought a couple of Napa Auto Parts stores, in Empire and Hughson. So I ended up moving back.

I changed my mind about small towns. I took care of all of our books, payrolls and tax returns. We divorced in 1993, and I went into real estate.

We had always bought and sold a lot of property. I was pretty familiar with the process. Of course, I was like a lot of people who think a great way to spend a Sunday afternoon is going to open houses and having a look at a bunch of homes. Anyway, it sounded like a very interesting field. I decided maybe I'd give it a try.

I had also attended a lot of my husband's sales functions and heard from several motivational speakers. I thought real estate was something I could do. I liked working with people, which is something I missed when doing my accounting work, where I didn't have as many face-to-face contacts.

With a 12-year-old daughter, I needed a way to support myself. I didn't want to be punching a time clock and be stuck at a desk like I was with accounting, the auto parts business and banking. And I knew I wanted to have some more flexibility to do the other things I enjoy.

There were 40 hours of training. Within three months I was selling real estate, starting in Oakdale in 1994. It is a nice town. I wanted to stick with a smaller town rather than Modesto. I knew eventually I wanted to live in Oakdale.

I thought Realtors® made a lot of money and didn't have to work much. I found out your time really isn't your own. When buyers call and say they want to look at a house tonight, I had better go and do it—tonight.

The funny thing is that of all the property I bought and sold over the years, I never had one Realtor® stay in touch with me when the transaction was done. You never heard from them again. I thought, "Gosh, if I stay in touch with people, eventually I may have a pretty good business built up here." That's pretty much how my business has evolved: from referrals and return business.

I was usually in my office first thing in the morning. I'd sit at my desk, listen to other agents I could overhear. I'm a strong believer in continuing education. I took every class I could find on real estate that the Central Valley Association of Realtors® offered. I took classes when the title companies offered them. This business is constantly changing and we have to stay on top of things. I made it my job to be more knowledgeable about the local market than any other real estate agent in the community.

And I concentrated on Oakdale.

I have horses. It's my other passion. So I concentrated on ranches and horse properties, and building up a clientele there. I also have traditional buyers and sellers.

I did some prospecting. I did a lot of open houses. I started a contact management program. In the beginning I kept an address book and constantly sent out post cards and notes to people. There were no computers back then for do it for us. I hand wrote addresses, probably 100 a month, and sent out personal notes. I read the local newspaper front to back. If I spotted a picture or an article about someone I knew, I'd cut it out and mail it to the person with a note congratulating them: "Your son (or daughter) was a student of the month"—that kind of thing.

It definitely paid off. People called. Integrity is very important. People have to feel like they can trust you. So you're going to be honest with them and give them advice. If you don't have the answer to a question, you'll get an answer for them in a timely manner.

I made it my job to know the inventory of homes in town that were for sale. Very often that gave me an edge in a listing appointment. One time I had a listing appointment for a million dollar home. I knew the people were interviewing several agents. Everyone did a market analysis of the home for the meeting with the sellers. I went out and visited all the comparables so when I met with them, I could say, "Here's a house larger (or smaller) than yours and it's got a barn." I knew about all the other homes and how they compared to this house. People would tell me they chose me over other agents because I knew about the other houses so much better than anyone else they talked with.

It's very important to pay attention to what people are saying. You ask a lot of questions and really listen to their answers. It tips you off about what they are really looking for. It's important to be able to communicate. Say for instance it's a couple; you communicate with each of them to zero in on the different personalities of each person. You may speak to them differently and also come to recognize which one is making the decisions.

As much as we're on the Internet today, it's still all about personalities and being able to connect with someone. I think lots of times we can overcome many obstacles if we have that human connection.

Growing up in the Valley, I always knew PMZ is the best real estate company. My family did business with them before. My mom and dad bought and sold through them. And I sold a house through them. I knew PMZ is the most visible company and that it's been around for a long time. But when I went into the real estate business I also knew I wanted to be in Oakdale and they didn't have an office there.

Over the years I got to know several PMZ agents as well as Mike Zagaris, whom I met at different training sessions I attended. "So when are you going to come to work for PMZ?" Mike would ask.

"When you open an office in Oakdale, I'll be the first one to sign up," I would answer.

I'd been thinking of making the change anyway. I worked for a great broker who was honest. But he was retiring, and also not very progressive; he couldn't offer the marketing and Internet pluses I could get at PMZ. I was starting to feel that I couldn't service my buyers and sellers more effectively without availing myself of PMZ's online presence and better marketing services. There were several clients I sent to PMZ.com to be notified when houses came on the market that met their criteria. Clients would tell me, "Wow, PMZ's website is the best."

I knew PMZ was the best thing for both my clients and myself, but especially my clients. Six months after the conversation with Mike, I was working for PMZ, probably one of the best decisions I ever made for my business.

One thing I prize is the reputation I have with other Realtors® in town for being honest and straightforward. If I tell them a house is available, they can trust me. They know I'm not playing games with them.

~

JOSEPH BONDI
'Becoming Your Client'

(Joseph Bondi is meticulous and thorough in how he takes care of his clients. See more from Joseph in Chapter Ten.)

I was born in Maryland in 1957, but we moved to Long Beach and I spent most of my childhood in Barstow, California, in the high desert of Southern California. There was very little to do there.

I wanted to get out of Barstow. So after high school and before the age of 18, I immediately went into the U.S. Navy, where I was trained as a dental technician and stationed, where else, at the Marine Corps facility back in Barstow.

When I got out of the service in 1978, I moved to Modesto in the great Central Valley. Low rents. Easy living. The movie "American Graffiti" depicted Modesto. I loved classic cars and owned a classic '58 Ford pickup truck.

After working at a couple of sales jobs—I sold vacuum cleaners door-to-door—I got a job as a chicken catcher. I was one of about 200 guys in 10 chicken-catching crews going through long houses at chicken ranches picking up the chickens to be loaded and shipped to market. I did that for six years.

I became a truck driver for the same company. They moved me up to assistant foreman for the trucking operation. Then a stark reality hit me: I realized I would never go further than I was at that job. I wanted something more.

As luck or grace would have it, the Realtor® who sold me my home, Pat Gray, came by one afternoon to visit. She had just opened her own real estate office and said I had exactly what it takes to sell real estate.

So I drove a truck at night and studied by day to get my real estate license. I took the test in 1985, got the license and went to work for Pat Gray in Ceres.

It was terrible. Interest rates were still high. The market was bad.

I also had a trucker mentality as opposed to a sales person mentality. I was driving a 1962 Ford Falcon Ranchero in 1985. I'd tell people my other car was in the shop. I didn't have money and was living paycheck to paycheck.

It was a difficult adjustment. I was going from very strong blue-collar work into a white-collar business job. I had the heart for it but didn't know how to dress or how to conduct myself.

After six months at Pat Gray's small operation I realized I would never really achieve my goal. Then I met Dean Russell, a real estate broker for a large firm in Modesto, who would become a father figure for me. I went to work for him in 1986.

He taught me not to be afraid to knock on doors—and not to

be afraid to tell the truth, even when it hurts in terms of getting transactions done. Don't lie, he taught me. Put it all on the table. He said when you get a bad reputation in this industry the news travels really fast. I like for people to know when I'm on the other side of transactions to be thankful they're working with someone who will do the job honestly and pay attention.

Dean Russell had this great phrase: "Play real estate tennis." What he meant was when you get paper work—or the ball is in your court—take care of it immediately and get it back to the other agent as fast as you can so it is in their court. It's such an efficient way of doing things.

I see so many agents who hold onto paperwork and don't quickly complete a task because they're either lazy or don't pay attention. It slows down the process.

He also taught me that real estate is a job. You come into work at 8:30 in the morning whether you have something to do or not. You treat it as a job. You put in the hours and it will translate into something.

Because of my work ethic, Dean told me, "Joseph, get here at 8 a.m. because the agent on duty might not show up until 8:30 and you can get the calls that come in between 8 and 8:30." I can't tell you how many transactions I got from being there early. There are some people who like to get things out of the way first thing in the morning.

When I had been with him for 12 years, Dean Russell semi-retired in 1997. I went to interview with Mike Zagaris. I knew PMZ was the strongest real estate company in the Central Valley. I had never met Mike but knew his reputation as a visionary.

I found out PMZ is very service-oriented for the agents as well as the clients. That was neat. The staff at PMZ fell over themselves to get me the things I needed to do my job. They made sure the phone lines were set up, business cards were ordered in a timely manner, announcements were sent out to past clients. And they did it all with a smile. It was always a pleasure for them to serve me.

I had a computer when I joined PMZ. Few Realtors® had one then. I shared my computer knowledge with other agents to encourage them to get computers. Mike was fast stepping into the 21st century. He knew what was happening with the Internet, e-mail and computer technology before the rest of us. He had the first real estate website in the city of Modesto and was willing to put together an IT department to help his agents.

Mike never made any requests of me because I already had a good work ethic when I got to PMZ. He'd have yearly goal meetings with each agent. At our meetings we'd talk about where I wanted to go during the next year. Usually my goals were pretty self-explanatory. He gave me suggestions and his blessing.

Over time, my productivity went beyond my wildest expectations. In my first year in the business in 1985, I maybe closed five or six transactions. During my 12 years with Dean Russell, my maximum closing of transactions was 56 or 58 a year.

I came to PMZ during a down market in the mid-1990s. Once the market picked up, I was with the number one firm with the best staff and technical support, advertising and company services—like in-house lending for clients to obtain their mortgages. That provided a great package that could not be matched by any other firm in the market.

There was only one way for me to go: Up. In the time since the market picked up, my highest closing year has been 2003, when I did 80 transactions with sales valued at more than $14 million.

What's behind my success? Well, first, all calls are returned. Period.

I don't make the mistake many agents make. If I get bad news and I think it can be fixed in a 24- to 48-hour period, I will bear the pain of the bad news and try to figure out a solution before I call the client. Let's say I'm representing a seller and find out the buyer has some difficulty during the loan process. But I'm not sure it will sink the deal. I don't call the seller and say the buyer may not get the loan. I wait for a day or two until I find out for sure. Often it gets taken care of. If it's going to get fixed, why have the client endure a sleepless night. Instead, I'm the one who loses sleep.

Another thing is I like to tell clients about my life. For 14 years I've been sending out special Christmas cards to clients with a story about how my year went. It talks about everything from the new car to my dog, whose name is Attitude, plus a little about real estate. When they don't get my card by December 15th, a handful of past clients will give me a call.

I get a lot of referrals from past customers because of my sphere of influence. People I work with on a professional level in real estate who are not Realtors® tend to use me as their own agent: lenders, pest control inspectors and contractors who work for many agents. They have a lot of choices, including Realtor® who produce more than I do. It is an honor to have them choose me.

I've come a long way in learning how to communicate. When you talk with people, you have to become your client. When I have a conversation with an older lady, I speak clearly and softly. I'm gentle. When I have a conversation with a trucker, I become the trucker, using tougher, to-the-point language. When I speak with a white-collar professional, I speak in the manner to which he or she is accustomed.

I call people with titles by their title. I'm working with a doctor now. I know his first name but I call him doctor because he's earned the title through his education and sacrifice.

When I'm with first-time homebuyers or sellers, I speak with them not as a Realtor® but as an educator. I want them to know what they're doing as they do it and after they've done it. I don't want anyone to trust me so much that they just take my word for it when I say you have to do something or when I say this is how things are normally done. I explain to my clients why things are done this way so they'll understand why I'm asking them to do it.

I tell my first time buyers and sellers that I want them to be so well educated that they'll be questioning me by the time we arrive at the close of escrow. People really appreciate it. The process can be a mystery and very intimidating.

It's great when I have a second-time buyer or seller who has had a bad experience with an agent who didn't perform his or her duties well. I love that. It's challenging to show the client how it can be done right.

I ask all my new clients if they have ever purchased or sold a home before and what their experience was with the last Realtor®. Boy, do they like to talk about the problems. My strongest suit is avoiding the problems they had before. My clients don't even know it's happening, but they love it. And it produces a lot of repeat business and referrals for me.

I figure that if they had bought or sold real estate before, they had known and worked with a local Realtor®. But they're working with me now. I ask myself why they're not working with that other Realtor® when he or she had the opportunity to be a lifelong Realtor® for this client. Why aren't they with that person now? The answer is simple: They weren't satisfied.

~

JILL SCHMIDT PARKS
'Anybody can be average'

(Jill is the daughter of legendary PMZ agent Phil Schmidt and a great agent in her own right. See more about her in Chapter Nine.)

Today's depressed market is frustrating for buyers and sellers. But I still like what I'm doing. We're just keeping it positive and keeping it fun. There's nothing better after writing 12 offers for a client and then seeing the buyer get what he or she was looking for and wants.

It takes that kind of effort. Sometimes clients want to throw in the towel and settle for something less than what they want just to get into a house. I feel at moments like that we're counselors. After we've been looking for a year, I'll tell them, "You can't do that." There's no satisfaction in it for me. After a year of making offers that don't go anywhere or after being outbid, I'm not going to give up, because I was raised my whole life with the philosophy that anybody can be average. It's easy to go through life being average. But you don't work hard to basically give up even if the buyer wants to give up and accept something less.

I need the reward of knowing my clients are happy. I don't want them to just say, "Jill sold me this home." I don't want to sell anybody anything they don't want. Even if it takes months or years, I don't care.

One sale took a year. Another I'm still working on has so far taken eight months. But at the end, the buyers are happy—as well as educated. They've seen it all, and they know the values and what they're willing to pay for something if it has everything they want. Even if I have to struggle through a dozen offers, I don't want only the husband to like it or for the wife to hate it—or for them to end up with a house they can't afford. I want them to be happy in the home and financially comfortable so they don't have to stretch it every month to make a mortgage payment.

I know people; I guess it comes from my dad. Some people tell me, "Oh, you're a mom. At least in real estate you can control your own schedule. You can come and go as you please." No, that's not the way this business works. It's more than a traditional full-time job, especially in this market but even when the market is booming. When something good comes on the market, you run for it. You've got to be there for the clients.

~

VICTOR BARRAZA:
'Paying attention to clients'

*(His is a remarkable story of success at a relatively young age.
Learn more about Victor in Chapters Four, Seven and Nine.)*

If I paid for advertising, it involved mailers, newspapers and off-and-on Spanish-language radio. But the majority of my business, now and in the past, comes from existing clients. A lot of my advertising consists of word of mouth.

One of the things that is different with me is that lots of real estate agents decided to go after the REO, real estate owned, accounts, meaning the banks or lenders foreclosed on the houses and own the properties. More than 90 percent of those selling homes are banks that own the houses and need to sell them.

Not me. I didn't go after those accounts. This was at a time when the market slowed down, between 2006 and 2008. I stayed somewhat busy, amassing clients I was working with and referrals that came my way. I just focused on taking care of my clients and did not go after soliciting REO accounts.

On one hand, I regret not making the time and effort to go after those accounts. On the other hand, the REO business will eventually dry out once the economy picks up and the market improves. That will absolutely happen. It's just a matter of time.

I know many agents who are heavily engaged in REO business and have not made any effort to contact previous clients. The REO business can keep agents very busy with all the miscellaneous tasks required, leaving little time to work or connect with other, more traditional, buyers and clients.

There is a lot of work, a lot more extra paperwork than your average listing, involved with REO accounts. It's the way banks are set up with their hierarchy of management. It demands more checks and balances to make sure things are being done properly. Banks want to make sure the list price is really accurate—as well as all the other things you're suggesting to do with the house—being as they're not actually there locally as your average individual homebuyer would be. Agents handling REOs may be dealing with someone in Dallas, Texas, who has never even been to California. The banks need constant updating on comparable sales. They also need your help. Sometimes when you list a house, it's presently occupied by the previous owners or tenants. You have to handle the process of getting the home vacant, coordinating cleanup and in some cases repairs, and rekeying the property—getting new locks installed. There is a lot more time and trouble associated with REOs than with traditional listings.

Because I have stayed in communication with previous clients and continued to make the time to work with them and the referrals they continue to send my way, I have succeeded in today's market even without the REO accounts. I have not only survived, I've done very well even in a very difficult market.

I've been through this before. It wasn't this extreme, but it was comparable in the early '90s because there were plenty of homeowners finding themselves upside down with lower home value to mortgage, and having to face the reality of foreclosure.

When you face that situation, whether you're upside down $20,000 or $200,000, it's still the same reality and the possibility of a foreclosed house. Back in the '90s, there were not as many people losing their homes as now. But it is comparable individually.

I've done well in today's market precisely because I've maintained good contacts and been available to my clients, their family members and the people they've referred to me. Since my large local client base has continued to expand, I've positioned myself very well. My clients will be around—and their referrals will be around—for years to come, even after the REO business is gone. I have positioned myself for the long term.

Lately, I've seen the largest percentage of my clients being investors. The second largest is first-time buyers. My smallest client group consists of those who are interested in move-up housing. There aren't as many of them right now. They can't afford to sell. The move-up buyer traditionally uses equity in the existing home to buy something better. They presently don't have much equity. Even if they don't need equity because they are tapping into their own savings, a lot of move-up homebuyers are unable to sell their existing homes.

The current down market is so amazing because it's gone on so long. But every real estate market offers its pros and cons, regardless of whether it's a booming market or one full of foreclosed homes like we have now where the values are really low. Even as gloomy as it is when you talk with people, you still have first-time buyers who are having the time of their lives right now. For the first time in a very long time, the affordability is at a level that is very accessible to most people who are in a position to buy. It is allowing many first timers to purchase their homes at a monthly payment lower than if they are renting. When you consider some of the government credits available for first-time buyers, if buyers are able to qualify for loans, there is absolutely no reason why they shouldn't take advantage of it. Most buyers will understand this and act on it when presented with the facts.

Other factors are low interest rates along with high rents, low prices and government help. We have such a good mix that it isn't so much about convincing people; it's about taking them through the process of what it will take to make it happen. In the majority of cases, if people can qualify for loans, they are going to want to do it.

Persuading people is really a matter of laying the facts on the table, doing a comparison of their costs of renting and their costs of becoming a homeowner, and having an honest discussion of the reality of the market and the changes we can expect to see. In most cases with clients, we can agree the market will eventually improve and home values will climb. This adds to the motivation for people to do something before some of the government assistance programs end or are curbed or prices start increasing again.

My client base puts me in a good position. I'm not bombarded with a ton of miscellaneous work on REO accounts. I'm able to take the time I need to spend with clients, making sure they understand what we're trying to do, what needs to be done and finding appropriate properties for them.

That's why when I saw what was going on with REOs, I decided I'm going to do what I do best, which is continuing to take care of my client base. Then, when REO accounts eventually dry up, I'll continue with a client base that will have expanded quite a bit.

The timing is working out very well for my investor clientele because we've got that right mix for them of low values and high rents. Rents decreased only a small fraction as compared to a short time ago. On the other hand, home values have decreased substantially. And so have interest rates.

This is the mix that investors look for. I have investors who have their home and want to buy a second rental property. I have investors who have purchased 8 to 12 properties in the last several years. They're still doing okay. Some of these investors bought recently when there was a positive cash flow and they were able to lock into some good properties with a mortgage at a great rate.

The current mix can blow me away. There's a Latino family living in a very moderate-priced home with three bedrooms, two baths and a family room addition put in a few years back. It's probably worth $85,000. The couple is in their 70s. The gal was still working in a local cannery until the last season or so. She just retired. The husband retired four years ago. I knew them from when we did a transaction together maybe 10 or 12 years ago. So they called me and wanted to look at a house close to where they live. I looked into it and showed them a property, an entry-level house in the $50,000 to $60,000 range. They wanted to buy. Low and behold, to my surprise they paid cash for it. It brings in about $1,000 a month in rent for them.

Right before they closed escrow, the same couple asked if there was anything similar around. I found them two other addresses of comparable houses. They bought them both. To my surprise again, they paid cash for both of them too. In the course of about a six-month period, they purchased about 10 houses averaging between $50,000 and $60,000, and paying cash for the majority of them. It's amazing that even when the economy is the way it is, there are some hard-working people who have been careful and saved and are now reaping the rewards.

My investor clientele, the biggest percentage of my customers, is still going strong. I have several other clients who recently bought four to six properties and are still looking for more. They're prospecting in this market. Think about it: If you have $60,000 in cash, it earns little interest, even in a CD account at the bank. We've been able to buy single-family houses at prices that produce $1,000 a month in rental income. If they finance them they can still write off the interest payments as well as the taxes. They're an excellent investment in today's economy.

I do some quick math: On $70,000, at a 4 percent interest rate, that's $2,800 a year, divided by 12 months is $233 a month. So if someone has $70,000 in the bank earning 4 percent interest, they're only earning $233 a month. Contrast that with purchasing a home for $70,000. Even after paying taxes and insurance, you're still making $870 per month with rental income. There's no comparison. That's what I get the majority of my investor clients to understand.

I have a mix of investor clients. Some are just starting off investing. Some are very well off. Several of them are following the same strategy by acquiring, in addition to single family, duplexes and fourplexes at entry-level prices.

So my focus is on the traditional value of paying attention to clients and building that base. Once I understand my clients' needs, it comes down to knowing what I know about real estate. I ask myself the question, "If it were me trying to accomplish the goals my clients have, what would I do?"

Meanwhile, I keep a diligent eye out for that property that will work best for a particular client. Once we find it, we take some quick action to get it locked in at the best possible price. That's why together with my clients we enjoy a lot of success.

∿

LANE MENEZES
'Finding the Right way to Communicate'
(He is known throughout the region as "The Ranch Realtor®.")

I was born in Patterson in 1959 and lived in Gustine, southwest of Modesto. My parents were dairy farmers and I was raised on dairy and farming. We moved to Modesto in 1967, while we continued dairy farming in the Westport area west of town.

In 1975, after my brother graduated high school, my dad said to my brother and me, "Boys, if you want to stay in the dairy business, I'll get more cows and build a bigger barn. If not, you go for outside work and I'm going to sell the cows." We said sell those cows.

After Ceres High School I went into the electrical business, working for eight years as an electrician doing remodeling work on dairy barns. Then I went to work for farmers, using my own equipment, a John Deere 12-row corn and bean planter. It created 12 rows covering 32 feet at a time.

I was planting beans for one of my clients in spring 1989. He jumped into my tractor and said, "You ever thought of selling?" I sold the planter to him.

I had wanted a career in real estate because of a relative who worked in a little real estate business who was just starting off. He asked my wife and me to come to a new agent orientation. He wanted to fill the office up with bodies. I went, sat down and listened. After the guy got through talking, I told my wife, "Annette, I can do this business and sell ranches for a living."

That fall I was running harvesting equipment for a friend. I ordered a mail order Principles of Real Estate course and listened to the tapes over and over again 18 hours a day while I was in the harvesting machine. When I took the test, I finished in an hour. I easily passed and got my license in February 1990.

I started at my cousin's little office in Modesto. I won all the top awards. I was selling big ranches. My business grew. No one could compete with me.

In 1993, I heard from Mike Zagaris. He sent out a packet of information concerning a small ranch in Escalon to about 20 agents to see if they could sell it. I sent him back a thank-you note for thinking of me.

"I want you to know I sent out packets to about 20 agents and you were the only one who sent me a thank you note," Mike told me. "I appreciate that. If you ever want to make a change, I'd be more than happy to sit and talk with you."

I thought it was time to make a change. I met with Mike and Phil Levin, sales manager for the Orangeburg Avenue office of PMZ. We sat down and I had 20 questions to ask Mike. Halfway through, he interrupted. "You know," Mike said, "I've never been interviewed by an agent. I always interview them."

"This is a big decision for me," I replied. "I want to make sure it is the right move."

"I understand and appreciate that," Mike said.

I made the move. Mike has an amazing mind, a way of translating his ideas and thoughts to anyone he talks with in a form that is adaptable to them. He saw my business and how I ran it. He gave me great ideas on how to put business together. Rather than invest a lot of money in advertising, I go out and talk directly to key people who help other people make decisions. Instead of a shotgun approach, I use a high-powered rifle to meet other people who buy and sell ranches. He supported me the whole way.

I was at the point where a lot of time was being spent on the road. I was averaging 150 miles a day. Now I find myself on the phone, putting deals together with repeat clients who keep coming back.

With Mike's help—through several meetings held over the year—I keep focused on the importance of talking to key people. He has helped me set the groundwork for a good strong foundation in the business that I didn't have before because I didn't have anyone with Mike's knowledge to bounce ideas off of. Other real estate gurus have great knowledge of the business when it comes to residential. But that doesn't apply to me because I sell ranches, not commercial or residential properties. My business is unique.

My volume has gone from $4 million in sales in 1993 to around $12 million a year now. My business has worked up to the point where it is consistent. Mike taught me how to keep it smooth and continuous.

I'm actually a very shy guy who doesn't like to go out and force myself on anyone. I prefer to have people call me and invite me in. It doesn't always work. But you have to communicate with people at a certain level. Mike gave me pointers on how to do that. He also suggested I take the Tony Robbins course.

It's a matter of getting on the phone and finding out what a person's needs are, listening to them and being able to help them without being pushy.

Some dairymen and farmers are very loud. When you call them on the phone while they're on their tractors, there's a lot of background noise.

They'll answer the phone and I'll say, loudly, "Tim."

"Yeah," the guy will answer.

"Tim, it's Lane."

Once that's all done, you can have the conversation with them. You can get so good at matching their sounds and tonality that you could be evil and lead people astray if you wanted to. You have to be honest with people.

A little old lady will say, softly, "Hello."

I'll say, also softly, "Hello, is this Mrs. Robinson?"

"Yes."

"Hello, Mrs. Robinson, this is Lane Menezes."

When it is an elderly person I'll often continue the discussions with a family member (who they feel more comfortable with) handling the matter. It works very well. You establish rapport.

The main thing is to get past the facade within the first three minutes. The person you're calling is wondering: Is this a sales pitch call? Is it a waste of my time? If you can get past that, you can do business with people because there is a trust that builds up. That's where people who are unscrupulous can take advantage.

Some years ago a dairy farmer called wanting me to sell his property. He signed a listing agreement with PMZ. As soon as it was signed, I immediately went out and within hours found someone interested in buying the working dairy facility. Then the dairyman had a change of heart—seller's remorse; he didn't want to sell after all.

I couldn't let the man out of the listing agreement because I'm only an agent; it was up to PMZ. So I spoke with Mike Zagaris. He said that I could legally hold the seller to the agreement. In the same breath he asked me, "What would you like to do?" If I wanted to pursue the contract, he promised to back me up.

I replied that the seller was not a sophisticated gentleman and I though it was the right thing to do to let him out of the agreement. Mike totally agreed.

The seller knew he was on the hook and was very worried about being forced to sell his property or facing possible legal problems. I knew he was sincere about changing his mind.

He was relieved when I told him I would tear up the listing agreement. As a result, real trust built up with the dairyman and he told others about what had happened. I've gotten business because of how I handled the situation and because Mike was willing to back me up and let me do what I felt was right.

This is a wonderful business. You can set your own hours and pattern. Mike Zagaris has been gracious enough to give me the reins to build up a business that fits my personality, which is not to work fast, but consistently and thoroughly. It is almost to the point now where I need to bring in an assistant in order to grow the thing a little more.

～

ROSE MARIE MENDONCA
'Giving personal attention'

(Rose Marie is a top real estate broker associate with PMZ and a legend in the San Joaquin County real estate community. Read more from her in Chapter Nine.)

I really work hard for each client. My goal is to get them the best buy there is for their money. It doesn't matter if they're rich or poor, young or old, white or black or whatever. I give them a lot of service.

After a while, I built up a lot of experience because I handled almost every kind of property there is around here. I have a lot of first-hand experience with houses, apartments and farming properties. I know the territory pretty well.

I really do give them personal attention. When I'm working with someone, they have my attention. I counsel a lot of people and have made a lot of people very wealthy. The word spreads around pretty well.

Before they're my clients, people come in for advice. I give out a lot of free advice. At least 30 percent of my time is spent just counseling people with all kinds of problems they have concerning real estate and business. Lots of times they aren't yet my clients. Eventually, they become my clients. They figure because I've done a lot of things, I know more than most agents do.

If you go practically anywhere, people are talking about real estate because they think there's money to be made in it and they're hungry for it. So everywhere I go, people want to know what the market is like, what's for sale, what's the future of the market and the economy in my opinion—all that kind of stuff. And I'm happy to share it with them.

When I started out, I was always asking people for their opinion of things. I admire people who are self-made. If I ever had a chance to talk with a self-made person, I'd talk their ears off because I wanted to know how it works. Others do the same thing with me now. I don't know why, but they do.

I don't advertise or do any promotions. I've been in my office for quite a long time with my name on the sign outside. I still am. My business pretty much comes from word of mouth. I get referrals from old customers, and now their kids. There are a lot of cases where I sold to parents and their children and now occasionally to their grandchildren.

~

ROSA GONZALEZ
'Being sensitive and caring'
(You can see more about Rosa in Chapters Two, Six and Nine.)

A lot of sellers in short sales don't get much sympathy. This was especially true at the beginning. But it is still real estate in a different market. All of a sudden, people don't have equity and the people willing to do short sales have to put their ego and pride on the table. That is so difficult to do.

By 2009 or 2010, when so many more people were going through the same thing, it was easier.

I never treated them as some sort of deadbeats. I treated them with dignity and respect. I adopted them, understanding the full dynamics of what they were going through. I incorporated that attitude into my exchanges with representatives of the lenders on my clients' behalf.

The hardship letter is one of the most important pieces of the short-sale package. It's the letter that gives sellers the opportunity to explain to the bank or lender why they are in this situation and why they need help. Sometimes what's in the letter is also communicated in personal conversations over the phone.

I remember one example that really affected me. She was a single mother of six children who at one time was earning a very good six-figure income. She worked for a lender, handling loans. Then the economy slowed down. She was no longer producing the numbers and she lost much of her income. She got behind and couldn't keep up with the house payments any more. It was the home of her dreams, a beautiful large house that she worked so hard to achieve for herself and her kids. But she knew she had to sell it.

Her children went to the same school where I used to work. She handled loans for the lender, so we saw each other at seminars and fashion shows. We were casual friends. When she needed help, she contacted me.

She was very emotional. There was a lot of crying when she told me about the position she was in: having to pay her bills not but making the income she needed. She couldn't keep her home. Especially being in the industry, she had given it a lot of thought and decided I would be the best person to represent her because she knew I would be respectful, diligent and professional, and do everything possible to get a successful short sale done for her.

Being in contact with real estate agents every day and doing deals with them, she wanted to choose the agent with the right personality for what she was trying to accomplish. She realized there is not a foregone guarantee that you can do a short sale. Not then and not now.

The first thing I told her was I would be very careful not to let everyone know about her situation. She didn't want her kids to know the house was up for sale. She didn't want a for-sale sign on the front lawn. She didn't want everyone to know the troubles she was facing.

Some of her concerns were against my better judgment, especially concerning the sign. I've always been told that's the best form of advertisement, and I've agreed.

But my job was to be present for her needs. I had to be sensitive and caring.

I listed her home, called the bank, said who I was and explained to this person that my client owed more than the home was worth. "Is it possible to do a short sale?" I asked. Not many were happening then. I was told that what was needed was a contract and an estimated settlement statement from the local escrow company—and a hardship letter.

First I had her complete a third-party authorization allowing me to talk to the bank on her behalf. I put her house on the market, listed it and did open houses. She would arrange for the kids to be out of town when the open houses were set.

I got multiple offers, took the highest and best, and did all the paperwork. She had to sign the papers. It was very emotional. This was her dream house and she was letting it go.

We got everything the bank wanted, including the hardship letter. My client and I wrote it together over tears. It was her words and emotions; I typed them out for her. (Now we know hardship letters are more effective if they are written by hand.)

The bank accepted the deal. The short sale was accepted as payment in full on the loan. She was able to walk away from the debt, which was a very good outcome for her.

It meant that my client had remained true to the commitment she had made when she got the original home loan. Then, she had committed to making the payments, which she took seriously. She didn't want to go through foreclosure. Making good on her promise meant behaving properly, both for herself and the lender.

She was relieved that there were people who really cared. First there was me, but there was also the lender that did the right thing in approving the short sale. The lender wasn't obligated to do that.

At the end of the short-sale process, there was a lot of crying and hugs. We are very close to this day. She owned an investment property, which was not her primary residence, and she also didn't want to lose it through foreclosure. We successfully did a short sale on that as well.

~

ROXANNE BAZUIK
'Doing an awesome job for clients'

(Roxanne, who shares her real estate practice with her husband Mike, also appears in Chapters Six, Eight and Nine.)

I'm not as disciplined as my husband, Mike, whom I partner with in our real estate business. That's something I'm definitely working on. It's one of my personal goals that I wrote out.

I'm in the office at 9 a.m., looking up properties to show clients at noon. I signed up with an REO (real-estate owned) company that handles bank properties. It will hopefully be a source of referrals for sales. I completed a course as an accredited REO agent.

Always changing markets mean new strategies need to be implemented. You always have to change because if you sit there waiting for the phone to ring, it's not going to happen. Too many agents just sit there waiting for something to happen. I've seen it.

People have different ideas on how their businesses should operate. We happen to be a little more aggressive.

Even in 2009, when it was getting tough, we still managed to close 91 deals between the two of us. We had a little bit of everything.

If you constantly sit there and think one thing works well and it will continue to do so, you might be missing the boat on something else that will be more lucrative for your business. I could sit there and only do buyer sales, but working with traditional buyers is not easy, even though I enjoy buyers. There's nothing better than getting a first-time buyer into a new home. That's very rewarding.

It's one of the biggest things people will ever do—buying a home.

I love being a part of that, especially first-time homebuyers, who are often younger couples, because they're so appreciative. They really appreciate you taking the time to get them into their first home, something many of them have long desired. So, being part of that is huge for me. A lot of people who waited and got priced out of the market at one time are buying homes later in life too.

When clients appreciate you, you appreciate them right back. People need help in real estate transactions. You instruct and help them become pre-qualified and pre-approved for a home mortgage. I don't show properties unless they're pre-qualified; otherwise, you could really be spinning your wheels and it doesn't make business sense. Once clients are pre-qualified, it's a matter of deciding together what they qualify for, finding out what their interests are in a house and then finding the right home—going specifically to the properties that will meet their interests.

I might have clients who are approved for between $150,000 and $200,000. So I try to show properties where prices are down to the $150,000 price point. Then, if those houses don't interest the clients, we can go up a little bit, find something a little bit better but still keep them within an affordable monthly payment. I don't want to get clients into situations they can't afford. I certainly don't want any of my people to end up losing their homes.

We work the numbers for our clients. I can pull out my calculator and show them then and there pretty close to what the monthly payments would be on a particular house. I always try to figure on the high side so they're comfortable with the properties we're looking at. "Wait a minute," I'll sometimes tell them. "We need to find out whether we can afford that." Sometimes you need to take two steps backwards. I think the work ethic is something we need to make sure we don't lose sight of so, it comes down to putting people in a home they can comfortably afford.

I don't prospect as much as my husband does. But I do prospect. One Saturday, I managed to make it to 11 homes, knocking on the doors of properties where the owners were possibly facing foreclosures. These are people who could be in trouble, could need information and could be sources for short sales.

It produced one bite, someone interested in checking out short sales. It's all a numbers game: The more people you reach, the better off you are. You're always going to reach a certain number before something breaks; no one knows what it will be. It could be that you talk to two people or 30 people to produce one real lead that can result in a listing and sale. That, in turn, can open up a new door to a referral lead based on the job you do for that client.

We get a lot of referrals from previous clients. I keep in touch with them on a regular basis. I'm better at that than my husband, Mike, is. I call the previous clients and ask how they're doing and if there's anything I can do for them. I ask if they know anybody who's interested in buying or selling. I do an awesome job for clients and they reciprocate.

Chapter Four

Effectively Communicating

Real estate is a people business. So it's really important that real estate agents weave themselves into the fabric of their community. A later chapter addresses agents giving back selflessly to the community in which they live.

But whether it's business or charitable activities, agents need to rely on all kinds of different means of communication with people. They are involved in face-to-face exchanges with clients, telephone conversations, mail, fax, email and online communication. But today, as this book is being written, we find ourselves in the midst of a social media revolution.

Agents need to pay attention to the power of using social media to develop and maintain their relationships with others. With that in mind, here are some stories from professionals who really know what they're talking about.

~

SARAH FIELDS
'From shoe leather to digital footprints'
(Sarah Fields is a social media expert as well as a real estate sales professional at PMZ.)

I have been in real estate for some time, starting in the title business, doing marketing consultations and working through title companies for real estate agents in business planning and helping them develop their marketing plans.

Born in Modesto in 1978, I'm a lifelong resident. My parents were involved in education and graphic design. My stepfather was an instructor in graphic design and the dean of vocational education at Modesto Junior College. After graduating high school, I went to the junior college for two years before transferring to California State Polytechnic University, San Luis Obispo, where I earned a B.S. degree in business administration with a marketing concentration in 2001.

Communications and marketing always were a passion for me. I watched my parents and their associates crafting their communication plans through graphic design and development of advertising. So I always had an affinity for marketing and messages.

I put myself through college as a food server in restaurants. Before that I worked at the college with my stepdad. He would have me develop communication pieces and help with marketing while I was still in high school. It was neat because it laid a great foundation for learning all the software I now use as the basis for developing messages; it gave me a strong basis in computer software technology employed in modern-day marketing and communications.

While in college, I participated in an innovative program called the Integrated Core Program. Instead of taking classes one by one, students came together to take all of their classes together. We found out how finance and marketing work together, how computer-based management information systems worked with human resources. They integrated concepts between individual classes and demonstrated how in business they all function together. So the end result was development of a fully integrated business plan. I acquired a strong interest in developing business plans for organizations and making sure all the elements of the plans function well together.

After graduating college I moved to Pleasanton in the East Bay, where Fidelity National Title Company hired me. I started working with sales representatives to develop their marketing plans and with lots of real estate agents in developing consolidated business plans so they could plan their objectives and the actions needed to realize them.

At that point in time, marketing by itself was price prohibitive. Getting out messages to a certain number of people required funds to reach those people. It had to be done through some form of print or direct mail. Television or radio advertising were very expensive forms of communication. I tried helping agents continue to consistently communicate with current and prospective clients in a fashion still within their defined budgets.

That led into what I'm doing today. Instead of needing to have money to get a message across or keep your face in front of prospective clients or extend your personal sphere of influence, through social media and a well-crafted online presence, you basically trade the financial investment with an investment of your own time and creativity. That's what I teach agents to do at PMZ.

In Mike's earlier book he relates a quote from Mike's father, Paul Zagaris, that the only thing that sells real estate is shoe leather. That means you have to hit the pavement and have your face in front of prospective clients in order to generate business and keep your business pipeline full.

With social media you're able to write an effective digital footprint. It's an opportunity to be present in front of the individuals doing research and spending time online to buy or sell a home. Or you meet them where they are: The sheer numbers from Facebook show 50 percent of its audience comes back every single day.

There are hundreds of millions of users on Facebook. Fifty percent of them log on every day. Average users spend more than 55 minutes a day on Facebook. More than 1.5 million local businesses have active "pages" on Facebook. More than 60 million status updates are posted every day.

Profiles of homebuyers and sellers show 90 percent of all buyers used the Internet to search for houses; 36 percent of buyers found the home they purchased through an agent while 36 percent (the same number) found the home they purchased online. Only 3 percent found the home they purchased through a print ad.

While shopping for properties, these homebuyers are encountering agents who list the properties and also end up shopping online for the agents they want to work with. That's why it is critical for agents to latch on in order for clients to discover them and evaluate them as a professional. Less is not more. As prospective clients use Facebook, Twitter, LinkedIn and blogs when comparing agents, the agent with the most relevant content available is essentially initiating relationships with clients before they've even met. Social media gives clients the chance to learn about agents and decide whether or not they want to choose them as their representatives.

All this just underscores the importance of populating the web with information about the agent since the client is online shopping for the property and will inherently research the agent at the same time. It also demonstrates the lessening value of print advertising and the need to compensate for this lost audience by offering information to clients through the Internet, where they are looking for it.

At a traditional meeting between an agent and client, once you leave the meeting you don't leave much behind. And there even fewer ways for you to continue to contact people who weren't even there.

If you are able to craft a strategy for utilizing social media, you have this opportunity to have scalable relationships, meaning now your interaction with prospective clients becomes scalable. Instead of going to meetings where you meet a finite number of people who happen to be there, now you have the chance to engage with a much larger population of people who are participating or meeting in the online social spaces. That allows you to dramatically increase your reach. Through this digital footprint, you're leaving behind a trail of your activities and information about your expertise and insights as well as giving clients the chance to know things about you that will let them connect with you.

Another element of the relevance of scalable issues taking place online is the fact you leave this digital footprint and it lasts until the targeted person comes in and is able in his or her time to engage with you. You can engage with clients or prospective contacts on their time.

In a lot of ways, social media has become the new form of direct marketing. In the past, real estate agents sent out newsletters with industry-related content and appeals to their audiences. There would be a calendar of events for the local community or recipe cards. The same types of communication are popping up in social media online through status updates and blogging or video posts or whatever vehicle agents choose. Through social media, agents can tap the same types of content as conventional mediums but also provide prospective clients with even more insight into their passion and professionalism.

I tell agents they need to share both their personal and professional insights. There's a time and place for everything. It's very important that agents select their networks or platforms based on their targeted audience. It might be a blog, network or video sharing site. It's then very important that agents evaluate their target audiences and within that space share relevant information.

So for instance, if the target audience is primarily business to business such as investors or commercial clients, agents should be in the LinkedIn social network because there is an understanding that it's for very professional conversations and content, endorsements and resume building.

Facebook is critical because it's really important for agents to go to where the people are and not just concentrate on technical innovations. Facebook is where the general population is because it has such huge appeal and participation. Personal profiles on Facebook are synonymous with participating in off-line social networking functions such as fundraisers or parties or some other forms of social gatherings. So the expectation is when in the Facebook social realm, you function in the same was as in any social environment.

So with Facebook, you want to take the opportunity to let potential clients know you're in real estate, but you don't want to spend your whole time talking about your listings or latest transactions or the newest changes in real estate regulations. Instead, you share of yourself in a fashion that gets your new contacts to trust you, be interested in you and connect with you.

Facebook has two kinds of accounts: personal accounts, which are traditional, closed networks where you have to be accepted as a friend in order to participate and it also has a professional-type page called the Fan Page, which It functions the same way as a website in that it speaks to the search engine so the content is searchable by Google, Yahoo or Bing (all search engines). In that space you can build it out like a website with all the relevant information about you and your business.

You can utilize space on your Facebook Fan Page to address the niche you've carved out for yourself. So let's say you have started a first-time-homebuyer-related Fan Page. This is like being at a professional networking event where people expect to gain insight about your professional expertise based on the niche you've set out.

With websites, you put information out and wait for people to visit. With Facebook Fan Page or with a blog or with Twitter, you are constantly populating the search engines with content to draw visitors back to your site so they can find more information.

One thing I tell people is when you attend a social function offline, like a fundraiser or socially-based event, you're only going to get as much value out of your time there as you put in. So if you go to a party and stand against the wall or in the corner and don't talk with anyone or share anything about yourself, you're not getting much out of it. The same thing happens online. The more you share of yourself and the more people you interact with, the more impressions you leave behind and the more productive it will be.

That being said, remember that just like being at an offline social function, you can't expect to walk away from the event with a deal. It's about building trust and relationships that will blossom later.

I've seen this process work well in real estate. Oftentimes, when you're searching the Internet for a topic involving someone's name, the first page results are coming from Facebook, Twitter and the blogs. The reason is because this is the type of content the search engines are looking for. They want fresh content that is the most recently updated. They also look for the longest history of content. So the more pages, or deeper content, you have behind you on your website, the more likely the search engines will recognize you as a credible source.

We have LinkedIn with a large audience of professionals. Your content there adds professional value to the network. One strategy you can utilize in LinkedIn is to pay it forward: Do for someone else before you expect him or her to do for you. One of LinkedIn functions is to generate endorsements that build your reputation and get the word out. Instead of waiting for people to offer recommendations for you, you go out to other contacts and make recommendations for them.

Many agents have prospecting or productivity plans that can call for making 20 new contacts a day. Traditionally, that comes from knocking on doors or getting your card out to a certain number of people each day. Your productivity plan should also include online social interactions. On LinkedIn, you can strive for making four recommendations for people a week in your network because that produces recommendations back to you and gives you a touch point in the same fashion as handing out your business card to the clerk at the dry cleaners. What you have done is make professional contacts within the social network.

The funny thing about this is when you hand your business card to the clerk at the dry cleaners, only the clerk knows you are in real estate. With the online social network, when you make contact with an individual, his or her entire social network is also exposed to you at the same time. That's how you do scalable relationships. Unlike the actions where you participate one-on-one offline, online you can expose yourself to an audience as big as your contacts' networks.

Another example I like to use is demonstrating the old versus the new ways—the whole shoe leather versus digital footprints. In days past you'd send a marketing piece to your clients. You might leave door hangers or hand out magnets with a calendar of events or mail a postcard about a new listing in the neighborhood or issue a newsletter with a great recipe—all because you want the piece to have some kind of staying power.

The chances that a client will take that printed piece and put in it her purse or carry it around to share with family and friends are not very good, no matter how good the recipe or calendar may be. The cool thing about populating the social networks and online venues is that when you have content that's relevant to your audience, the audience can in fact share it with its networks by hitting the "share" link or by just commenting on some platform about your piece or post. Then the content gets shared directly with all their networks. You end up with a very portable content that potentially can go viral, meaning it can be shared indefinitely with extended networks. And best of all, it's free.

The piece you post on your blog or social network costs you time, but not a dime, whereas those printed pieces can cost you not only the time to create them, but the often-considerable expenses of developing, producing and distributing them. So in many cases for no charge at all—and just a modest expenditure of time—you can get a lot more exposure.

Understand platforms will change. Facebook is the number one social media in America. But it doesn't devalue the fact that agents have the opportunity to use Facebook in extending their reach and expanding their personal sphere of influence in order to capture clients and contacts today, then plug them into their databases and continue working with them as platforms evolve. You want to continue using Facebook as well as other direct marketing methods or networks. But as the deals and relationships are made, you translate them over to use in whatever new networks are next. If you capture them as clients and enter them into your own database, you continue communicating with them in other ways.

A lot of people make the mistake that because they understand how to use social networks for personal purposes, they think they are ready to use them for business. It's really important to remember you're using a network like LinkedIn as a professional tool. So it is crucial to have a well-crafted business strategy as part of a marketing tool so you aren't missing opportunities.

The first step is acknowledging you need a strategy. As you expose yourself to education about online tools, then you can develop an effective online marketing plan. Just like with traditional marketing plans, real estate agents have to carefully consider their objectives: What is the purpose for participation in the social network?

And they have to carefully consider their target audiences. Take a look at the profile of past clients to define target audiences so you can determine the networks that are best for them. Find the networks that address the kinds of people within those demographics. Then be able to effectively determine what type of information will be of value to that target audience.

I begin by asking PMZ agents to run through a curriculum with me. I start off with social media planning. From there we take a look at their objectives and target audiences, and then identify the appropriate platforms with them. We also take into consideration their own passions, personalities and interests. So if you have particularly charismatic agents, they may be good candidates for video blogging, called vlogging. If the agents are hyper professional, love the business side of what they do and don't like to participate much in social communications, they may be better off with LinkedIn or a professional blog—or just sticking to a Facebook page. There is a platform for you depending on your interests and your level of social ability.

Also, given the target audience, agents have to develop a content plan—what the target audience wants to see or hear or what they find of value—and then give that to them.

Once a plan is in place, agents select the platforms and start digging in to start maximizing their presence on the platform. I tell them it is critical to go deep and not wide. So they don't want to have a light presence on 20 different networks. They're better off having deeper connections on just a couple of platforms that appeal to the specific audiences that are being targeted.

In terms of having the best life—and fulfilling Perfect Day principles—I love to share with agents a way to structure their social media engagement without letting it take over their lives. For example, part of what I work on with agents is allocating a specific amount of time each week to using social media and giving them specific objectives to achieve during that time. Then it becomes part of their managed prospecting efforts, just like spending a certain number of hours a week placing prospecting calls on the telephone.

The elements I suggest incorporating into this social media prospecting time slot each week are the following:

1. Expanding your networks: Allocate, say, 10 minutes on each of three days a week for social network prospecting. One part of expanding the network is committing to making 10 new connections a week.

2. You also want to participate in generating your own relevant content at the same time.

3. Engaging your own networks: Comment on, replying and reach out to participate in other people's spaces like writing recommendations for LinkedIn, commenting on someone's Facebook post or replying to a tweet in Twitter.

The idea is no matter what platform you're in, practice these three elements: Extending your network, providing valuable content and engaging with your audience.

~

DANIEL DEL REAL
'A new generation uses social media'

(Daniel was named one of the top 30 real estate agents under the age of 30 by Realtor® Magazine. For more from Daniel see Chapter One.)

I was inspired to get into real estate by witnessing the example of my parents who succeeded with little or no formal education. They knew and know hardly anything about computers or high tech.

Now there is a new generation of agents who are utilizing social media to market and communicate with clients. There is a new generation of buyers who go online to do everything. So I know I have to go online too. That's our generation: instant gratification, wanting information and others' opinions.

I have a website at PMZ, which all agents can have. I have my own separate website too, which is about branding myself, making myself to be more of a brand. When people hear the name Daniel Del Real, I want them to automatically think real estate. That's my goal-www. danieldelreal.com-being in the real estate industry. It's worked for me—another source to generate leads and market myself. Everything is linked, to PMZ's website and to my blog and my Facebook page and my LinkedIn account. At the end of the day it all comes back to the same location.

My blog consists of stories and testimonials from my clients and myself. Mostly I post the stories myself. If I close a buyer transaction, I put up a brief description of how it got to me, how the search went, what the client wanted, how long it took to get them there, what they got, what they purchased, what the monthly payment and interest rate is and if there were any closing costs or concessions. You can see it all on one blog entry.

This does many things. It puts you in front of the new generation buyer. You're 23 or 24 years of age, and you think this is a good market in which to buy a house. Someone tells you about me. You come to my website and come to recognize yourself on my blog. You don't know what to expect, but because of the stories on my blog, you can read different buyer accounts and find at least one you can relate to—a story from someone like you. You want a house in Modesto for under $150,000. You see on my blog that someone bought one eight months ago. This was the price. This is what the buyer negotiated in closing costs. This is their monthly payment and interest rate. You say to yourself, "That's exactly what I want to do and where I want to be. If that person can do that, I can do that too."

Instead of hearing people talk theoretically about what they want, you can read real-life stories with real numbers and even see a picture of the house. Everything becomes real while you're reading my blog. And I've just become a value to that client, and he or she calls me.

You could be a first-time buyer or an investor. I put stories about my investors online too. With them, I include—in addition to the purchase price and interest rate—what their return is on the investment: the difference between the monthly payment and the rental income.

I had a Bay Area investor who purchased four homes from me. When he found my website, at first he didn't know the kinds of investments he could buy or the rates of returns on them. But because he went to my website and saw four to five stories from investors with terms that excited him, he called me and became a client. For him, hypothetical stories about opportunities in Modesto became real because of the genuine stories and actual numbers on my blog.

A lot of my clients are what I call the next wealthy generation because the investors, the young ones from ages 23 to 30, who are soaking up the market now will become the next generation of millionaires. When there's blood on the streets, there's lots of opportunity. Investors take advantage of that. There are a lot of young real estate investors purchasing homes.

I show buyers examples not only on my website but with what I've done through my own investments. I lay them out in front of my clients as well. These are my out-of-pocket expenses and my rate of return, I show them. It helps me establish credibility when they see I'm also doing what I'm preaching. The reason I do it like this is I remember once wanting to invest in the stock market. One of my instructors told me, "If you want to invest in the stock market with a broker, wouldn't it make sense for that stockbroker to show you what he's doing instead of just telling you what investments are out there?" So I only trust my money with people who are already dong what they are telling me to do. That's why I also put my own stuff—my investments—up in front of my clients. It demonstrates my trustworthiness and shows them I'm not just talking about investing—I'm actually doing it and showing them why I'm asking them to do the same thing.

It all comes back around to why I got into real estate in the first place. I'm doing now what my parents showed me they were doing when I had just gotten back home after my military service. And they did it with a fourth-grade education.

～

VICTOR BARRAZA
'There's been a transformation'
(You can learn more from Victor in Chapters Three and Seven.)

When I started in real estate the majority of my clients were Spanish speaking. I enjoyed working with them. It was comfortable. I felt like I excelled at it. I felt that was my perfect fit because I was able to learn about the business and learn about the process—everything about how to deal with real estate. It was also very pleasing. It gave me a lot of satisfaction to take these opportunities to Hispanic families in an honest and professional, way from which they could benefit.

The comfort and satisfaction came because honest bilingual real estate agents were a rare thing at that time. I thought I was filling a void. Then, my age played a role too. I would talk with people on the phone and everything went great. We'd meet and they'd wonder about how comfortable they would be with someone as young as me helping them out on something as important to them as buying a house. Working with Hispanic families, who were close to 80 or 90 percent of my clients, let me learn and gain confidence.

But time went by. Things started shifting. I started helping a wider variety of clients. The shift also went to where I wasn't so aware or self-conscious about my age, although a lot of people initially brought it up. As time went by and I felt more comfortable with what I was doing, it became easier to open my horizons to anyone and everyone, and to go after business that was not just comprised of Hispanics. I think 50 percent of the people I still help out are Latinos. The other 50 percent are a combination of Anglos and other minorities.

The shift changed my way of doing business. Years back I had to get up to speed on technology by using computers and emails and technology in general. Lately it's been using websites: Facebook and the miscellaneous other avenues that are available. What I use the most now are my own website and Facebook account.

The Internet makes information available and accessible. I'm able to quickly update information and promote the fact that this information is available online. It's also changing because more and more people are comfortable going online to help satisfy their real estate needs. That wasn't the case as much seven or eight years ago. There's been a transformation. It's amazing how many calls we get because people saw information about me, a house they're interested in or available programs such as short sales, refinancing and mortgage products like modifications of loans—all the different things available these days that people are interested in.

Online programs help people evaluate the situation concerning their homes. If they're curious about what their homes are worth, there are options on my website. I have links to government agencies for different programs that also provide specific information that fill people's needs.

Chapter Five

Being Present

Jon Kabat-Zinn wrote a book about using meditation to focus our attention on the present moment rather than the past, the future or the countless distractions that assault us in our every day lives. Here's how he began his book.

Guess what? When it comes right down to it, wherever you go, there you are. Whatever you wind up doing, that's what you've wound up doing. Whatever you are thinking right now, that's what's on your mind. Whatever has happened to you, it has already happened. The important question is, how are you going to handle it? In other words, "Now what?"

Like it or not, this moment is all we really have to work with.

You don't have to practice Zen Buddhism to appreciate Kabat-Zinn's message. You just need to be focused on whatever you're supposed to be doing at any particular moment in time.

I have learned the hard way the importance of being present in each moment of my life. I have discovered that when I'm able to focus on whatever I'm doing at any point in time, I generally produce great results. But when other things distract me, which sometimes

Wherever You Go, There You Are:
Mindfulness Meditation in Everyday Life, Jon Kabat-Zinn, Hyperion, 1994.

happens, my productivity drops dramatically.

One of the traits of great sales people is their ability to be present for their clients whenever they're communicating with them. Agents who get distracted by text messages or cell phone calls when they're working with clients lose rapport with clients—and too often at the end of the day, lose their clients.

The same principle applies during our nonworking hours. When agents are spending time with family, they need to be present with family, not thinking about all the pressures at work. I know it is impossible to perfect this principle, but we can make significant strides in coming close to achieving this end.

Here are a few stories of agents who are members of our team who I really admire for their ability to focus and be present in the moment.

~

TIM RHODE
'Switching channels'
(You will read much more about Tim Rhode in Chapters Six and Eleven.)

I strongly suggest people buy and listen to the tape series by Dr. Fred Grosse, "Black-belt of the Mind." Around the same time I went to Tony Robbins' Life Mastery course, I went to Dr. Fred's training. He taught me about a lot of the concepts I embraced. One of the best ones was what he called switching channels.

When I'm at work prospecting, meeting with clients or solving tough problems, I'm not thinking about my vacation, the mountains I love to be on or any other distractions that can take me away from giving the situation at hand the serious attention it needs. So while I am at work, I'm on the work channel.

As soon as I hit the garage door opener from my car, I switch to the family channel. If my mind tries to take me off to the problems at work, I don't let it. I might talk with my wife about what happened at work, what my day was like or a problem I'm having. She may be able to help some. But this is the time when I give my undivided attention to my wife and kids, and the rest of my family. I spend a full day at work, laser focused on what I need to do. I leave at around 5 p.m. Then I absolutely turn work off and I'm done with those thoughts for the day.

By the way, you'll never catch me at the water cooler talking about last night's "American Idol" television show. That just doesn't happen. Sorry, I don't mean to be unsocial. I just have My Big Why—where I want to go with my career and life—that I'm working on there. I'm not at work to make friends or be part of a social clique. My focus is, how can I work the least number of hours, get the most amount of work done and spend as many hours as possible doing the wonderful things that make up a great balanced life.

When I'm coaching other real estate agents, which I like to do, I try to help them be the most EEP they can be. That stands for efficient, effective and productive. One thing I feel I excelled at was being efficient, effective and productive in all areas of my life, and especially in listing and selling real estate—and using every hour of the day to the fullest in order to be able to be successful. I'm also that way when coaching Little League for my son, being there for every parent-teacher conference at school, being a vital and fully engaged human being and being a productive member of my community.

~

AARON WEST
'Being in the moment with clients'
(He has succeeded by focusing and building relationships.
Learn more from Aaron in Chapter Nine.)

Staying focused is something I have really concentrated on since I first got into real estate. Real estate taught me patience. My previous career, 10 years working in sales at Rogers jewelry stores, was about instant gratification. If you did a good job, the customer bought something right then and there. I had a very short attention span. Being in the moment is one of the issues with most sales people, or people in business in general. They're always thinking of what they will say to a customer or how they will respond next to what the customer may say to them. They are not necessarily focused on listening to what the customer is saying.

It's not much different in real estate. Most agents—or a good number of them—are thinking of what they're going to say next to make that client want to work with them or to get the client to do what the agent wants them to do. The agent is not necessarily sitting down and really listening to what's important to the client. It's one of the reasons I've really systematized things when I meet with clients for the first time. I already know what I'm going to cover in our first sit-down. Then that allows me to focus on what the clients have to say and learn what's important to them. This lets me be in the moment with the clients. I lean forward and listen to them. Then they know I really care about what's important to them. It's not that I'm just selling them a home and then they'll never hear from me again. I want to be that agent who five years from now they may turn to if they want to sell their home. There won't even be a decision-making process; they'll just pick up the phone and call Aaron.

Because at the beginning I stay in the moment—I really listen to and understand the clients—it tells me where they're coming from and lets me work through the whole process with them so they are confident I'm looking out for their interests. A lot of people think a real estate agent is someone who shows up to make the fast buck and then gets out. Being able to separate myself from that stereotype has really made a big difference in growing my business.

Chapter Six

My Big Why

"Your old men shall dream dreams, your young men shall see visions." President Kennedy was fond of quoting that passage from the Book of Joel in the Old Testament as he described the need for more freshness and imagination in approaching public service and world affairs. It applies equally as true today in any number of endeavors.

Many people spend too much of their time daydreaming about what they'd like to see happen. Creating a clear vision that actually makes things happen is an entirely different matter.

I've been fortunate to know and work alongside a number of extraordinarily successful individuals both inside and outside real estate. What I find in each and every instance is that the lives of these accomplished men and women are ordered around a precisely articulated vision of the future. That vision is unique in each and every case, but in each case it represents a compelling picture of the future that each person has forged. That picture is so bright and strong that they are drawn towards it. That vision affects what they do every day in such a way as to become self-fulfilling.

Everyone deserves to have such a compelling vision, what I call My Big Why. Everybody's Big Why has to be customized to that individual and speak to his or her innermost ambitions and wishes. For those fortunate enough to share their lives with another person—a spouse or significant other—it's important that the development of their own Big Why be accomplished with a sensitive respect for the aspirations and desires of that person.

There are a number of people who really understand and have applied these principles who are highlighted in this chapter. I need to offer special recognition to Tim Rhode, who helped show me the value of developing a Big Why in my life.

~

TIM RHODE
'Creating my own life by design'

(Aside from being one of the most successful real estate agents I know anywhere, Tim Rhode dedicates himself to educating and mentoring new generations, both in real estate and other fields. For more on Tim, visit his website, www.1lifefullylived.org.)

Your journey must start with a long-term vision of where it is you see yourself down the road. In my vision, I'm sitting for a family portrait. I'm 90 or 95 years old, sitting with my spouse and our kids and their kids, surrounded by children, grandchildren and maybe great-grand children. I want to be sitting there with my wife wearing a big ear-to-ear cheesy grin.

In order to get to that place, I have to have done a lot of things right. I have had to take care of my body so I'm still there physically. I have had to have a great relationship with my wife so we're still together. I have had not to run out of money. And I have had to have my family still loving me and still wanting to be part of the picture after all those years.

That means I have to exercise and watch what I eat so I'm still around and healthy. I have to not fool around on my wife or she'll leave me. I have to be wise with my money or I won't be smiling in the picture. I have to keep a great relationship with my family members so they want to be in the picture too.

I attended classes with my wife over 21 days given by Tony Robbins, the self-help author and success coach, called "Life Mastery."

When I took those classes I was chain smoking, overweight, not as successful in my work and in kind of a rut. What I realized was I wasn't where I wanted to ultimately be in life. That was in 1997, around the same time I first met Mike Zagaris.

Tony Robbins helped me create a vision for a 10-year road map of where I wanted to transition my life. He helped each person in the classes pose the question to themselves, the same question I now often ask my fellow real estate agents to ponder: What is your My Big Why?

It can mean different things for different people. My Big Why is the life I find myself living now that I wanted for myself 14 years ago.

I work because I choose to work. But I also make time to get to the things I love the most. I call them the "ins": skin', hikin', bikin', rikin'. Riking is something I invented. It's when you hike up a big hill with no snow and use ski poles to run back down. It's a form of exercise. There's a peak behind my house called Riker Peak, which I named. So I invented my own sport and named my own peak.

I literally created my own life by design. I had a vague vision of this life back in 1997 and continuously upgraded my plan until eventually executing it approximately in 2005. This vision, or My Big Why, is what got me up every single day passionate to do the things I didn't want to do, knowing they would eventually lead to the life I'm now living.

In each of us there is what I call a committee, a bunch of different people all grabbing for attention in our brain. At different times it's appropriate to have different people in charge. When I'm skiing, there's a 12-year-old in charge. I let him take the lead then. However, when it's time to prospect or make that phone call and that kid tries to step up and say, "I don't want to do this and you can't make me," the all-knowing adult inside of me tells that child, "Shut up, you're going to make the call." This is what I have to do.

I suggest that what all agents do is physically write out My Big Why and have some sort of end goal in mind. It's the road map to making it to where you want to go. In my life, it was a long-term 10-year vision plan that I call a Marathon Plan. When I first set mine, I decided 10 years from now I wanted to be living in the mountains and doing my "ins": skin', hikin', bikin' and rikin'. Maybe for you it's having the money to send your kids to college 15 years from now. It's different for all of us. But whatever it is, the end goal must make sense to you.

~

BEN BALSBAUGH
'Personal and professional success'

(A top manager and agent, Ben is one of my most valued colleagues. He set up PMZ's Carpenter Road office in Modesto and its Stockton office in 2002. See more from him in Chapters Seven, Eight, Nine and Ten.)

Twenty percent of real estate agents traditionally do 80 percent of the business. That's probably true of any sales operation. Today, with the market being so bad, it's probably closer to 15-85 or even 10-90. Today's challenge is that we see lots of agents doing everything they can to make it into that upper echelon. Spirits are down. It's hard for people to wrap their minds around a strategic plan because all they're focused on is feeding the family and making ends meet.

It doesn't matter where you're at today. You have to get together a road map. It applies not just in Stockton where I work, but everywhere. We're trying to lift spirits, to give people hope. That's why My Big Why and My Perfect Day are so relevant.

Even we managers get wrapped up in our day-to-day struggles. I still try to do some sales and focus on my sphere of influence: people I've known and served over the years. I want to continue helping them with their real estate needs.

I also try to look in the mirror a little. Then I ask myself how much of what we preach about My Big Why and My Perfect Day do I actually live every day? I think I do a pretty good job, but I can do better.

I originally did My Big Why about six years ago. I didn't call it that then. I've written out financial and relationship goals every year. Paul Harmon, my colleague at PMZ, and I surround ourselves with folks, mentors who are successful and challenge us to be the same. We search out and pick up those tools.

But My Big Why went from being driven just by money—financially driven—and shifted to being successful personally as well as professionally. That's been the lesson I've taken to heart lately.

Overall, I have been pretty successful. When I was a senior in high school, working at Costco and starting at $8.25 an hour, that was a huge deal. It was well above the minimum wage then. I've always been blessed with a good job and being surrounded by good people. And I've always strived to make it to a higher level. I think it's about a mindset.

People struggle, especially today, to see light at the end of the tunnel. How do I get from here today, when I don't seem to have anything going, to there tomorrow where I can achieve some level of financial success?

I grew up in the country. We didn't even have a television until I was 12 years old. My brothers and I were always outside playing or working on the ranch with my dad.

People will tell me, "Ben, you've never hit bottom. You've never known what it is like to do without." Well, maybe that's true. But if it is, it's because my father instilled this work ethic in us.

It was all about hard work and discipline. My parents didn't have much money when I was young, but we kids didn't know it. My dad worked so hard, he always provided. After moving out of the house, I looked for other business leaders whose examples I could learn from.

~

PAUL HARMON
'Inspired to succeed'
(For more from Paul Harmon, see Chapter One.)

I've always written down my goals. It goes back to a trait I inherited from my mom, also a top real estate agent for PMZ. It goes back to when as a fourth grader I earned $1,500 over the summer months to buy a three-wheeler motorbike by working odd jobs. All that made powerful impressions on me. You set a clear goal that you want, you create tasks to accomplish it and you set off to make it happen. I'm not a one-page goal guy. I'm a seven-page goal guy. I've created these categories, each with a set of one-year goals. There's "Thinking Big," a spiritual category, a family category, a financial category, a business-personal development category, a relational category and a physical category. I review each one of these pages each day. I look for what I did today to accomplish those goals. I look at what I will do tomorrow to reach them.

An example is that one of my relational goals is to be an encourager—to tell people what I am thankful for about them. For instance, my wife and I have a date night once a week. So I remind myself to make sure to have that date night. Under business-personal development, I read a book a month. I actually read six over one two-month period.

Also under business-personal development is the goal of being progressive, which is the ability to challenge your mindset, which can make you feel uncomfortable and awkward at times.

There's a spiritual goal: asking how God can use me in a bigger way; a family goal: taking more day trips with the kids; a relational goal: having no regrets; and physical goals: working out five times a week, living more healthy this year and taking daily supplements.

So often, all people want is the big pill, the overriding goal. But how did you buy your big house on the hill? Did it happen overnight?

It's the chipping away at it—the small goals you accomplish daily and the goals you accomplish weekly and monthly that all add up.

What's more, too often people look at the mechanics of things and don't examine the emotional side. You have to be inspired to succeed. You have to tap into your emotions. If not, you won't be consistent in your daily, weekly, monthly and yearly efforts.

Moreover, your goals have to include the welfare of others as well as yourself. I'm currently on the board of Sierra Vista Child and Family Services, helping women and children who are in need, from clothing to food to shelter to counseling. I'm also on my church's financial planning board; we help members of the congregation with counseling on budgets and personal finances. I'm a past board member for Community Hospice and the Alumni Board of Directors for California State University, Stanislaus, my alma mater.

I'm still very active as a volunteer with my church and in other organizations. And I go to all my kids' games, which is one of the reasons I decided to undertake a career in real estate.

~

MEREDITH BRANDSMA
'Holding yourself accountable'
(Hear more from Meredith in Chapter One.)

I absolutely credit My Big Why. It's interesting because I never did it before. I always considered myself a goal-driven person. But I guess they were more short-term goals that were in my head. I knew that this is what I needed to do or wanted to do in the next week or month. I didn't ever sit down and lay out my long-term goals: What do I want to do in my life over the next year or over my life's work?

I've always found goal setting a little daunting. When I was in the non-profit corporate world, the part I hated the most was long-range planning. I'd sit down for an entire weekend with 20 board members and figure out long-term goals for the organization. It was a constant struggle. Nobody had the same ideas or wanted to go down the same path. It was difficult. Perhaps that's why I've always been a little reticent.

But not long ago, when Mike Zagaris challenged and encouraged me to do this, I finally sat down and did it. Mike gave me a formula that suddenly made all the sense in the world out of My Big Why. The formula was to section or divide your life into four different parts and keep the listing of all your goals to one page, no more than that.

I liked it because it incorporated goals from work but also things I wanted in my relationships plus how I wanted to treat myself and, of course, the financial part of my life. It was more of a plan for life than only about my work over just the next year.

So, for example, I sat down and took a good look at my relationships, one section I set goals for, and examined what I want to do over the next year: How do I make them better? I kept the goals specific. Rather than writing that I want to continue to have better relationships with my parents, I actually wrote that I want to communicate every few days with them, specifically more with my father because my mom and I tend to talk a lot and he often gets left out of the mix. What is nice about Mike's formula is I can set specific, attainable goals that don't feel overwhelming.

I just kept most of them to one year. There are a few areas where we're encouraged to think of goals that go more into the future. I went a few years out with some things, trying to think a little more in a big- picture way. But for most things, I thought about outcomes I want to see over the next 12 months.

What's also interesting about this exercise is that since I write the goals down on paper, I actually feel more compelled to do them. I feel like I'm holding myself accountable.

I placed the goals into a Word document and printed them out. Now they're up on the refrigerator at home and by my computer in my office. I see them when I get up in the morning or while I'm working. I briefly look at them and say to myself, "Yes I'm doing these things I set out to do."

As real estate agents, we can get so busy at the office with the many small things that come at us on a minute-by-minute basis, it's easy to get sidetracked. But with these goals hanging up by my computer, I can glance at them and say, "Oh, right, I'm supposed to be contacting someone from my database on a daily basis. Take 20 minutes and look at that database and give a past, potential or current client a call, or email him, or her or work that database as I challenge myself to do in my goals."

I started this process at the beginning of 2010. I've been pretty consistent. It has already paid off to some degree—and it's been very interesting for me.

One of the first times I fulfilled my goal of working the database, I called a past client who I knew had been somewhat interested in going down the investor flipping route. That's where the client purchases a home, fixes it up, turns it around and sells it. I came across his name in my database and gave him a call. "Are you still interested in this?" I asked. "It's not a bad time to consider it. Homes are at an all-time low as far as inventory goes. There isn't a lot out there for first-time homebuyers." As a result, he purchased two homes and started flipping them—fixing them up. They were listed within a few weeks.

I'll keep at it. I think it's great for work—and great for myself. It tends to bring some balance into my life. It reminds me there are other things I want to do other than work. I might not otherwise sit there and think of some new things I want to try with my life, to learn about. Once I put them down on paper, suddenly I'm being held accountable ,and then I tend to explore them a little bit more than if I hadn't written them down.

This process of actually sitting down and putting things down in writing forces you to really think about things in general. What do you really want? It helps identify who you are. That can only help you when it comes to your job. As an agent, it is important for you to know who you are, what you do best and how you operate best. Until you can identify those things, you can't become successful, at least not financially. Then your clients like and appreciate you and keep coming back to you. That's what I found most helpful about this process.

When I went through the divorce it slapped me in the face. I was shocked. I had no idea it was coming. So I had to sort of step back and all of a sudden take care of myself emotionally. I looked at my life and said, "I need to do something just for me." I took up equestrian activities—jumping horses. Mentally I needed to have some balance: I needed to have work going well and home life—and relationships—going well too.

It's easy to get away from that balance, to let it slide. It is easy to let yourself become unbalanced. It's an ongoing struggle. We never achieve perfect equilibrium. When you put it in writing, it does help you say, "Oh, gosh, that's right. I was going to do yoga every day, but I fell down on that one this week." It enforces discipline.

I will say I'm not quite so militant as Tim Rhode when it comes to the workplace. I like chatting now and then with coworkers, finding out how their weekends went. I'm not at the office to play around or spend time looking at my personal accounts. I'm there to do my job. I feel I've typically struck a pretty good balance between work and home life.

~

ROSA GONZALEZ
'You don't get anywhere without a plan'
(For more on Rosa, see Chapters Two, Three, Nine and Eleven.)

I was born in 1963, in Norwalk, California. My dad was a business owner and entrepreneur, and also sold real estate across the border in Rosarita Beach, in Baja California, Mexico. He came to the United States with no money in his pocket and worked at a metal finishing company for the architectural industry. He ended up owning it and opened two more offices for the same company, in Northern California and Mexico.

Growing up I wanted to be an interior designer, but after finishing high school in Norwalk, I went straight to work for the family business from 1981 until 1992, and moved to Stockton when my dad opened the Northern California plant there. He never wanted the company run by outsiders; he wanted it run by family, if possible. So when my husband and I got married in 1983, we moved to Stockton to run the business.

We did that for nine years, until 1992. It was great. I loved it. I constantly stayed in touch with family running the other businesses in L.A. and Baja California. Working with my husband, who also worked for my dad's company, was wonderful. That's how I met him.

The company shut down its Northern California location in 1992; the city of Stockton was so tough on us with its regulations. Both city and Cal-OSHA regulations made things astronomically expensive.

I got a job working as the principal's secretary at a private K-8 school my kids attended, and did that until 2001. I loved the kids, teachers and everything about the school.

Jerry Katzakian is the real estate agent who sold us our house in 1992. He saw what I was doing running my dad's company at a young age—how I handled everything. He came to the office to have me sign documents for the purchase of our home. I had an office staff and 200 employees in the shop then.

Jerry told my husband how really impressed he was with me and that when he was ready to hire an assistant, he would offer me a job. He thought I'd be good working for him.

One day we got home from work and Jerry's business card was on the door. We thought he was prospecting for clients so I didn't call him back. He came again when my husband was at home, saying he wanted to offer me a job. We had lunch. My husband and I agreed we'd accept because I was ready for a change—so long as it was the same or better money than what I was making working at the school.

It turned out to be better. So I went to work for Jerry as his executive assistant in 2001. It was just me. I coordinated his transactions and managed his database while he prospected all day; I didn't show properties, but I did everything I could do without having a real estate license. I opened escrows, did disclosures and talked to other real estate agents and clients, updating them on what was going on. I did everything I could so Jerry could stick to his schedule and focus on prospecting so he could grow his business.

This went on until November 2003, when I got my license and became a real estate agent on my own.

I made up a business plan, which I learned how to do from Jerry. I also attended a seminar, where I learned that you aren't going to get anywhere unless you have a plan. I had to know what my goals were—what numbers I was trying to achieve and why.

So I started putting together a plan of action. It said I would close 20 deals during my first year in business. My goal was to work with buyers to get my feet wet and to prospect for listings.

That's what I did. I closed my first deal during my first 45 days as an agent.

～

KAREN SERPA
'Getting there'
(Read more from Karen in Chapter Three, Nine and Ten.)

I do a lot of goal planning toward the end of the year, for the following year. Mike encourages us to do that. It's really important for me.

I really love what I do and love helping clients accomplish their goals. But I didn't really define my own goals, my own My Big Why.

I've definitely been thinking a lot about it lately.

Annually, at the end of the year, I write out what I accomplished that year. Then I write out what I think I will accomplish for the following year. This is where my business will come from and how it may change. I come up with goals to achieve, including what I need to do, how many calls and appointments I need to make each week and what are the community activities I need to attend.

Unfortunately, I'm not as detailed about it as Tim Rhode, but I'm getting there.

~

MIKE BAZUIK
'Making goal setting a way of life'
(See more from Mike in Chapters Two, Nine and Eleven.)

My mom, who was in real estate, started me on setting goals. I've probably had goals almost my entire life, from the time I was a little one. When I first moved out of the house, my goal was to get a condo. Another was to get a truck or motorcycle. I wanted a boat or to buy that house.

I have always supplemented my 401k or retirement plan. My goal for the last few years was to max it out at $42,000 (for self-employed SEP-IRA). To do that, you have to make $200,000 a year. Therefore, I had to have a goal to make $200,000.

Even at age 20, my goal was to contribute $2,500 to my Roth IRA toward retirement.

For me, goals seem to be a way of life. If you don't think about a goal and put it right in front of you, you'll never try to achieve it. Then it will always slip away.

At the end of the year, I usually sit down and write down some simple goals. I keep them in front of me every day, taped on the wall right near my phone.

I constantly remind myself of what was on a list I cut out of a daily business newspaper after they interviewed very successful people: How you think is everything. Always be positive. Think success, not failure. Be aware of negative environments. Decide upon your true dreams and goals. Write down your specific goals and develop a plan to reach them. Take action; goals are nothing without action. Don't be afraid to get started; just do it!

Never stop learning; go back to school or read a book or get training and acquire skills. Be persistent and work hard; success is a marathon, not a sprint. Never give up. Learn to analyze details; get all the facts, all the input. Learn from your mistakes. Focus your time and money; don't let other people or things distract you. Don't be afraid to innovate; be different because following the herd is a sure way to mediocrity. Deal and communicate effectively with people. No person is an island; learn to understand and motivate others. Be honest and dependable. Take responsibility.

~

ROXANNE BAZUIK
'Doing careful planning'
(Roxanne is also in Chapters Eight and Nine.)

You have to write everything down and decide exactly what you're going to do. In setting our goals, my husband, Mike Bazuik, and I don't go too far out. We usually limit our plans to a year at a time.

Right now our goal is to attain a new property for ourselves because we've been in the same home for 13 years and we want to acquire two rentals for financial freedom so we can retire. We had seven at one time. Now we have two. But two isn't nearly enough since we have to create our own retirement, being self-employed. So we need properties to generate income.

We need to acquire at least two more rental properties that we fix up and keep.

We have to write down our goals and see if we achieve them.

Generally, we do. It's been tougher because the amount of money we need to save to buy the three properties is high and we need to keep our payments affordable so we don't get ourselves into a position where we can't keep what we buy or properly maintain the properties.

You have to do careful planning. We have a 10-year goal to retirement but have to plan it step-by-step, year-by-year to achieve it. Sometimes there are goals to achieve in a shorter period of time—a three-month period.

There's one goal that I wanted: a cruise for the whole family-kids, spouses. My husband took us on the vacation because I won the competition we maintain between us.

We have a picture of our lake house glued to our printer. It's a view from our deck looking out onto the water at Clear Lake. The goal is to get it paid off, but having the picture up is also kind of soothing so we can look forward to being there. In a couple of days we get to go up there again.

Chapter Seven

Thinking Big

Thinking big.

Too many in real estate don't do it. They earn perhaps $20,000 a year. They must pay both the employer and employee sides of Social Security. They might as well be unemployed. They make far less than they would receive at a regular job.

The top 20 percent of real estate agents collect more than 80 percent of the income produced by all the agents in the business.

One of the characteristics that distinguish those who are successful from those who are not is that the highly successful agents all think big.

My understanding of the power of thinking big came through exposure to my father and to a great inventor and entrepreneur, Alejandro Zaffaroni.

Although my dad grew up poor and obtained much of his education a mile underground as a coal miner, he always thought big—both for himself and his children. He would consistently encourage each of his four children to think big and to think positively.

He taught me the concept of leverage. This included both financial leverage—how to control large amounts of assets with modest amounts of money—and more importantly, leveraging my personal power-how, although I am only one person, I can achieve extraordinary results if I think big and appropriately organize myself.

After graduating with a Bachelor of Arts degree in economics from the University of California, Santa Cruz, in 1970, I went to work at an entry-level position with a company in Sunnyvale called Xidex Corp. A spin-off of Memorex Corp., Xidex manufactured specialty microfilm products for sale to government and large businesses. After a few years and a number of promotions, I established a sound career path at the firm. It was a good company with good people. But I didn't find the environment very stimulating.

On a visit home to see my parents in Modesto I ran across an issue of Fortune magazine, to which my dad subscribed. It featured an article about a pharmaceutical research and development enterprise called ALZA Corporation and its founder, Alejandro Zaffaroni. Zaffaroni co-invented the oral contraceptive at Syntex Corporation and at ALZA pioneered the development of drug delivery systems such as the skin patches that are in widespread use today.

The magazine article about Zaffaroni and how he was such a big thinker and visionary was impressive to me. Upon returning to the Bay Area I decided to immediately seek out and obtain a position with his Palo Alto-headquartered company, which is now a division of Johnson & Johnson.

My thinking was simple: I wanted to be around people who were big thinkers. His ideas—and his work—completely transformed the manner in which drugs can be delivered to the human body.

I secured a copy of the *Palo Alto Times* and searched the employment want ads. There was a position open in production planning at Zaffaroni's firm. I applied, was hired and had a marvelous experience there for five years.

Among other things, I got to know Alex Zaffaroni. The exposure wasn't disappointing. Alex really did think big. He wasn't satisfied with thinking on the margins of life. He wanted to think big thoughts—and he did. I came to truly understand what one person can accomplish when he or she thinks big. The excitement, opportunities and success available to those who think big make all the difference in the world.

I also learned other important lessons. Alex taught me about the concept of perceived value: If you believe in what you are doing and the benefits of what you have to offer, then you can create greater perceived value by those who buy your products or services.

Among other things, ALZA pioneered development of drug delivery systems: innovative ways of delivering a variety of existing pharmaceutical products into the body for improved therapeutic results. Alex was able to convince the marketplace that the value of the innovations associated with ALZA's work was so great that his products oftentimes sold at prices that were 10 times or more above the competition.

In addition, I learned you cannot accomplish things you can't visualize. Embracing a frame of mind that recognizes the unlimited potential of a particular endeavor is to free yourself to accomplish much more in the real world than you would otherwise believe possible without those big thoughts.

I've become convinced that the real estate profession is a 100 percent mental business. It doesn't require physical labor of any consequence. The performance of people in real estate has to do with the conversations they have in their own heads; it is a mental game. If a person's mindset is focused on negativity, pessimism or limited vision, then the results will reflect those limitations. Most people don't draw upon but a fraction of their mental capacity.

Thinking big is a conscious choice. It is a liberating activity, which for people in real estate opens up their minds to opportunities that do exist. It makes it possible for them to create and execute meaningful plans that reflect their true potential.

Choosing to occupy this mental state is very important. You can decide how you view the world. You can decide whether to think big or to think small.

Too many real estate agents are conditioned by their parents or their upbringing, through their own experiences or by the people with whom they choose to associate, to see all the obstacles, problems and restrictions in the world. All that does is limit the potential that is out there.

I have seen it time and time again. We get a lot of people attempting to break into the business who have had drilled into them all their lives the notion that life is a struggle and the odds are they're not going to be more successful than their mothers or fathers. This inhibiting view often comes from well-meaning family members. Sometimes people have a spouse or significant other who doesn't want them to take risks. They fear the loss of security that a regular paycheck represents. They just don't realize that the only security any of us has is found within ourselves.

When you go into business for yourself you have to believe in yourself—and think big. If you don't believe in yourself—or you are not capable of thinking big—then real estate is the wrong business to enter.

People in our field also need to have a good self-image. They need to have that healthy conversation with themselves.

My theory is that we all encounter negative events and influences in our lives, obstacles that must be overcome. To be successful in real estate or in life it is necessary to take proper note of the negative factors and then learn how to let them go. Holding on to too much negative energy seriously limits the ability to adopt and maintain a positive mental attitude.

Some people endure genuine tragedies during their lives and are able to surmount them and become successful anyway. The question isn't whether you encounter adversity. The issue is how you deal with it. There is much merit in the old adage that says some people look at the glass as half empty and some view it as half full. Those who are successful in a real estate career see the glass as half full, despite the fact they are looking at the same reality as those who see the glass as half empty.

So not only do you need to think big, you must also think positively.

A healthy mental landscape is necessary for another reason. Sales is a people business. Real estate agents are involved with people all the time. The clients with whom they work quickly recognize agents' mental states. People selecting agents are looking for positive, upbeat, dynamic individuals who are confident in their ability to get the job done. If you don't exhibit a healthy mental attitude and a good self-image, or if you don't believe in yourself, then no one else will believe in you either.

Prospective clients are not drawn to do business with a real estate agent whose thoughts are dominated by his or her own personal difficulties and problems—someone who exudes a pessimistic viewpoint. Most clients see it and choose not to work with that agent.

However, I know pretty quickly when I'm in the presence of agents who believe in themselves and in their ability to sell—people with a big vision of their own future. I am very likely to want to work with those agents—and so will their clients.

You see, having a positive mental outlook is not only good for you personally. Having a healthy relationship with yourself significantly impacts your external relations with other people and enables you to achieve far more as a real estate sales professional.

Listen to the stories of just a handful of the agents with whom I have been proud to be associated.

~

BEN BALSBAUGH
'Striving for something more'
(See more from Ben in Chapters Six, Eight, Nine and Ten.)

While finishing my senior year at California State University, Stanislaus, I had a job at Costco pulling carts from the parking lot. I worked my way up to cashier, then front-end supervisor managing the cashiers. After graduating in 1996 with a B.S. degree in business administration and marketing, I wrote a letter to the regional manager of Costco looking for a management job. He called me and we met in the East Bay. A week later I was sent to San Jose to be a department manager for Costco. I was only 24.

I was there about a year. One day I woke up, went to work and while doing inventory late at night observed that all the other managers, my colleagues, were older than me. "I don't want to be doing this job at age 35 or 40," I thought. So I resigned and moved back to Modesto.

I had no plan for what to do. So I became an advertising rep at the *Modesto Bee*, the city's big daily newspaper. I didn't have any experience but got the job and worked there for two years.

In my second year I bought a domain name called CentralValleyJobs.com. Mike Zagaris called, saying he was interested in purchasing my domain name. I was interested in real estate. So I sold the name to Mike and went to work for him. While waiting for my real estate license, I recruited companies and posted jobs on CentralValleyJobs.com.

I became a sales agent at PMZ's Orangeburg office and spent a year and a half selling from my cubicle. Mike saw me work. He had me manage a new facility for PMZ, a big one, on Carpenter Road in Modesto. I started recruiting agents and building the office. When I left there three years later, it had gone from zero to 70 agents. Today, it has grown to 110 agents after adding more space.

Two and a half years into the Carpenter Road position, the job of setting up the new office was coming to an end. Mike said he had bought land in Stockton. I went there to set up PMZ Real Estate, from scratch. I had grown up in Modesto and knew people there. In Stockton, I didn't know anyone. But I built relationships. I weaved myself into the fabric of the community.

The Stockton operation went from nothing to 95 agents after five years in two large office buildings. I've been blessed to be around good people—that's the key: Good people attract good people. We surpassed our competitors and PMZ is now the biggest real estate company in Stockton. We want to grow it to 150 agents there.

~

CHRIS SHAW
'Achieving the potential I always thought I had'
(Chris Shaw is one of PMZ Real Estate's highest-performing agents. Get more from him in Chapter Eight.)

I was born in Oakland in 1952 and raised in Hayward, where I went to school. My father was self-employed and owned a successful tire shop. He retired at 46 years old. Then he got into real estate investing, where he was also very successful, buying and selling both residential and commercial property. My grandfather was a real estate broker in Hayward, starting in 1935. Real estate is in my blood.

After high school I went into the Marine Corps for two years before college. The Marine Corps matured me. I learned a lot. Boot camp taught me how far someone can push himself to achieve a goal. Without that I probably wouldn't be as successful as I am today. It's like cross-country distance running; until you push yourself to a certain point, you don't know if you can go there. Once you do that, you know nothing can stop you.

After getting out of the Marine Corps, I graduated from California State University, Hayward with a B.S. degree in business with an emphasis in accounting. I graduated in three years, going four quarters a year on the G.I. bill.

After two years managing my uncle's tire store, I entered real estate. I had 26 relatives in the tire business, but the idea of being self-employed, of controlling my own destiny, was drilled into me since I was a little boy. I wanted to be compensated based on how hard I worked rather than on a scale everyone else was making for a particular position.

So in 1978, I got into real estate after receiving my license. A year later I became a real estate broker. It requires an additional examination; the state waives the normal two-year time period you have to be in real estate to get a broker's license if you have a college business degree in a real estate-related field.

I opened my own brokerage office in Hayward in 1979. It was a struggle because the recession hit in 1980. I basically had to support the running of the office myself to keep the doors open. I had 13 agents, but they weren't very successful. That recession—with 20 percent interest rates—lasted until 1982.

You had to adapt to what was possible during the recession. Getting new financing was not an option then. Essentially, when we represented a buyer we had to search for sellers willing to carry the loan themselves or allow their loan with lower interest rates to be assumed by the buyer. Otherwise, people couldn't qualify or afford mortgages with 20 percent interest rates.

To get around the high rates I became an expert in creative financing—learning how to put transactions together where buyers would assume a first mortgage from the seller's existing loan. Then the seller would carry back a note that my office would sell to another party at a discount so the seller would be able to obtain most of the cash out of the transaction. It was like a second mortgage but without the bank and its high interest rate. Still, it was very difficult to find sellers willing to do this.

During this time it would take writing up and presenting about 30 offers to get just one accepted. My goal then was to write an offer every single day of the month to make sure I had one seller willing to accept. Eventually I'd find somebody.

This is how I really cut my teeth on real estate—when we were facing such difficult times and tremendous obstacles. I had young children to support and had to just go for it.

The brokerage operation kept going until 1982. Then I decided since I was basically supporting the whole office by myself as the broker, I might as well work on my own and not support all the agents. I became an independent real estate agent, handling the brokerage affairs myself.

The obstacles we faced became an advantage because they taught me a couple of things. First, they taught me about creative financing—and financing is the key to real estate. Nobody pays cash for properties. We always need financing. I learned about financing much more than any real estate agent does today in the business.

Second, I was forced to immediately size up a buyer to determine whether he or she was a viable candidate to work with because it required so much effort to get a buyer into a house, I could not afford to work with someone who wouldn't be successful. I was looking for the buyer's commitment to see it through—to see if they were willing to work as hard at it as I was. I devised ways to gauge their motivations, their ability to finance and how willing they were to accept properties that maybe weren't their dream homes.

I took those three criteria and placed them on a scale of one to 10. A perfect score would be 30. I worked with at least three buyers at one time who ranked highest on that scale. This took the personalities out of it. Sometimes agents like to take on a challenge and search for some property that is very difficult to obtain. The buyer's criteria is so specific that it might take six months to find this home where three other agents were unable to. Many agents, especially younger ones, try to save the day and find this perfect property for a young couple they come to love.

I made that mistake too when I was young. You work for months and months and can't find the property. Then I changed, and it became a numbers game for me. Because times were so tough, I chose to work with people for whom it was most likely that I could locate properties in the quickest amount of time.

The same is true today. Unless someone is referred to me, I leave the difficult challenges to other agents. I try to work with the best-motivated, financially able people who are willing to look at alternatives.

As an independent agent in Hayward after 1982, my plan was to simplify my life and work lean and mean with not a lot of overhead.

For four years beginning in 1985, my dad and I started an additional business in the East Bay purchasing foreclosed properties, fixing them up and selling them. We averaged two properties a month. There were a lot of opportunities because of the recession. It was very profitable.

Shortly thereafter I moved to Modesto. I wanted a different environment for my five children. They were growing up in the Bay Area where I didn't care for some of the influences. We moved to Modesto because it had a Midwestern flavor to it. The first day after the move we walked into a grocery store and a bank, and people said hi to us. That was not the case in the Bay Area. It felt very comfortable.

I went to work as a real estate manager for a homebuilder in town that also had a real estate office, Grant Realty. Eventually I rose to become vice president in charge of sales and marketing for the entire company, both new homes and re-sale homes.

Then I went to work for PMZ Real Estate in 1992. PMZ was the number one company in Modesto. It offered a home for experienced agents—and had the most successful agents in the area. I wanted to associate myself with those types of people.

My income had reached a plateau for the last few years before coming to PMZ. I had sort of achieved a comfort zone and didn't really know why. Maybe I thought this was what my level was going to be.

So I took a chance in going to PMZ because I knew the agents there were more successful than I was at the time. I figured there was no reason for that. They weren't in the business longer than I was. I didn't think they were any more intelligent, hard working or talented than I was.

But there was something lacking where I had been, or there was something they were gaining from PMZ.

At PMZ I found myself surrounded by successful people. Mike Zagaris led them. He was the most intelligent, forward-thinking real estate owner I had ever met. He was talking about developing computer skills at a time when computers weren't really utilized in our business. And he stressed setting goals.

All the agents had to meet with Mike on our goals. The first time we met I tried impressing him with goals that had no accompanying business plan on how to reach them. He clearly saw through that and told me I had to have a plan. He agreed to meet and help me formulate a plan to promote my business and develop my skills.

My best skill is that I'm a terrific salesman. I'm good with people. Mike and I determined that if I was going to increase my business I had to increase the number of opportunities to get in front of people because my batting average, as Mike likes to call it, is extremely high. I just needed more chances to increase my sales.

To better promote myself, I increased my advertising budget, especially in newspapers, in an effort to increase phone responses that I could convert into sales.

My income has increased every single year since I've been at PMZ. I hit my goals each year. Mike encouraged me to set goals that pushed the envelope but were still realistic.

In year one, 1993, my goal was to hit an income of $75,000. I achieved it, finishing with $80,000 that year. It continued to go up each year, in most years dramatically. Last year I made $539,000. This year I'm on track to exceed that.

About five years ago I decided to set my goals in terms of both income and the number of completed transactions. My goal was to eventually hit 100 transactions a year. I haven't quite hit 100. Two years ago I hit 98. Last year I did 99. I feel confident my goal will be achieved.

When I was growing up my father made $100,000 a year. I always said if I could make $100,000 a year, I'd be very successful. I went from earning $100,000 a year to $200,000 the next year and it has been steadily increasing since then.

Why the success? I'm at the highest echelon of this company. I associate with very successful agents. I'm a master at controlling my thinking, not letting negative thoughts interfere with my work.

So much of our success in real estate is tied to how we think, whether we are positive or negative. I'm able to control my thinking. When negative thoughts come in, I'm able to put them away in another part of my brain to deal with later and not let them interfere with my work.

No buyer is going to employ an agent unless they become friends with the agent. You have to become friendly and make friends with the client. No matter how technically skilled you are or how well you know the market, nobody is going to buy a house from you unless they like you.

Negative people are not likeable, certainly not for someone who is choosing an agent who will help them make the largest purchase of their life.

So controlling one's thinking is really key.

The other thing that happened to me when I came to PMZ was that after so many years in the real estate business, I had really become tired and complacent. At one point I was looking at getting into another occupation.

At PMZ I just embraced the business. I focused on goals, and when I achieved success it allowed me to strive for more success because I liked the feeling. By accomplishing those goals I also found myself achieving the potential I always thought I had inside me but for some reason couldn't reach before.

I learned some new skills too. Mike uses the analogy that real estate agents are like actors or athletes. The profession requires skills, and you have to practice your skills. Actors rehearse. Baseball players take time in the batting cage. We have to rehearse our skills too, so when it's show time, when we're on, we can do the best possible job.

On a day when I have an important appointment with a key buyer or seller, I will frequently take long showers and mentally go through my presentation, anticipating the objections I might hear. The difference between successful agents and so-so agents is the successful ones are able to isolate objections and overcome them. That takes learning questioning skills—asking open-ended questions to get people to talk and really reveal their concerns and interests.

There are studies that show the more clients talk, the more they like you. When I was in a sales presentation as a young agent, I liked to talk and talk and talk to show people how smart I was. I'd eventually wear them down.

Now it's a whole different process. Now, when I'm making a presentation, I take inventory at various points to see who's doing most of the talking. If it's me, I'll stop and ask questions, even if it's about a non-real estate topic, just to get my client to talk.

It really works. It's a matter of them embracing me and trusting me. When I feel it's time for them to make the decision, I'll structure an open-ended question that is compatible with the other questions I've been asking: "So, Mr. and Mrs. Smith, what are your thoughts on moving forward here? What are your thoughts on taking the next step in buying this home?" as opposed to "Do you want to buy this home?" where they answer yes or no. When I ask an open-ended question, it forces them to talk and explain and reveal their true feelings.

Then that tells me what I need to do. If they're ready to buy, we proceed. If they have questions or concerns, my job is to isolate their objections. So I'll say, "Tell me what's holding you back?" And they will. If they don't, I wait for the answer. I make them answer. Sometimes I have to repeat the question. But if I've built up the right kind of rapport, they'll answer it.

Finally, from the time I show up for work in the morning until the time I leave the office, I'm focused on my task. Many agents kind of work at half speed. They will spend time socializing because there is no boss immediately over them saying what to do every minute. I don't work that way.

People who punch clocks work from the time they get there until the time they leave. If all agents had that same sort of dedication, it would increase income by at least 20 percent.

I'm extremely disciplined. There is nothing that will stop me from achieving my goals. Part of that is what I learned in the Marine Corps: being disciplined, having a mentality that no matter how difficult the problem, I won't quit.

~

VICTOR BARRAZA
'Setting Goals for Yourself'
(See more from Victor in Chapters Four and Nine.)

I was born in 1969 and raised until the age of nine in a small town in the Mexican state of Durango. My parents were small farmers on their own land. From before I was born, my father came to the United States to work as a farm worker under the Bracero Program. He went back and forth across the border to provide for our family. At age nine, my family—five brothers and two sisters and I—migrated to Modesto.

My dad did farm work, picking crops like tree fruit and strawberries, and working in dairies. During summers the whole family worked in the fields, except for my mother and the small children. I remember working from the time I was nine, picking cucumbers, cherries and strawberries—and slicing open apricots before they were dried and shipped.

When my two years of junior high school ended in Modesto, I was one of two students receiving an award for perfect attendance, not missing a single day of class. Until I received the award, I didn't realize how rare that was. I assumed everyone had perfect attendance.

At Thomas Downey High School in Modesto, I ran track and

cross-country and got involved with the Azteca Club for Latino students, serving as its president when I was a senior. I graduated in 1987.

I worked throughout high school on a newspaper delivery route to earn extra money. At 15, during the summer, I worked in the local canneries canning fruits and vegetables, which was better than doing field work. During high school and for two years after graduation, I got a job at Rico's Pizza while attending Modesto Junior College. I started out as a busboy, then made pizzas and later became the manager.

At community college, I took the usual prerequisite courses. I always thought I'd have a career in art, which I enjoyed tremendously.

Instead, I got into real estate in 1989. I was intrigued by watching late night television infomercials promoting the buying of foreclosed properties, fixing them up and selling them at a profit. I was trying to convince my brother to go halves with me to buy the books and tapes for this course, costing about $400. At the last minute we did not buy the program, so it didn't go anywhere.

Then an independent Realtor® who was a regular customer at the pizza parlor told me how well I would do in real estate. He told me I should get into it. He spent time helping me to learn the process.

The term ended at Modesto Junior College. So did my job at the pizza parlor. I immediately went to real estate school, putting in 10 or 11 hours a day. I was able to go through the entire course very quickly. I took and passed the state exam, obtained my license and went to work with Ken Martin, an agent in Ceres.

Soon I was working with a larger broker, Grant Realty, which lasted for a year and a half. That was a great experience because it was the first time I was part of an organized real estate office. We had staff meetings. There were several other agents in the office to talk with. It was great belonging to an organization. Later I worked for Re/Max of Modesto.

Soon I was taking additional real estate training courses offered out of the area, in Sacramento, San Francisco and Southern California, including those by Mike Ferry. They drew people from across California and out of state. I was trained in many areas of real estate, including being goal oriented.

It made an incredible difference. One of the key things that keeps me on track throughout the year is creating goals for myself, making sure they're clearly written out and keeping my goals in front of me at all times. You have to make sure they push you but are at the same time realistic and attainable.

During the first six years I was amazed when looking at my numbers. Every year I did between 170 and 175 percent more than the prior year in sales volume. The numbers of transactions I closed set my goals. They kept increasing as the years went by.

I started my first full year at more than 20. After starting to take the training courses and adopting the goal setting, I moved up to 50 or so a year. Then it went from 56 to 70-some. It reached as high as 118 closed transactions.

One year I was tied for first place among all the Re/Max agents in Northern California, which covered from north of Bakersfield to the Oregon border. That year I had 86 transactions. Richard Damagalski, a fellow Realtor® also now at PMZ, was the agent I tied with.

That got me pumped up. The following year I did 102 transactions, expecting to win first place at the company. That year a bunch of agents started hiring two or three agents to work underneath them and counting everyone's volume as one. So the guy who won that year had 150; I was bummed. Soon afterwards I found out he had two licensed agents plus an assistant working with him. So for the last eight years, I've had a full time assistant.

Re/Max was sold to new owners. I had been contacted by PMZ on a few occasions to see if I was interested. I talked with agents who worked at PMZ to get their feedback before going there.

Mike Zagaris is a very astute investor and business owner. He has a great vision for the future of the company. He connects with people. And for someone in his position, it impresses me that he takes time to discuss things with his agents one on one.

I've also moved into investments. I bought properties, residential, commercial and agricultural. I currently own 12 residential units on eight properties, including duplexes, plus three commercial buildings and two agricultural properties—almond and walnut orchards—that are managed for me.

In 1991 I began a Spanish-language newspaper, *El Sol*. It is now owned and operated by the *Modesto Bee*.

Why have I succeeded? I think it has to do with my overall background, my work ethic, the fact I'm willing to work the long hours if that's what it takes, and finally my very supportive wife, Marisela.

I really believe my father and mother built a good work ethic in my siblings and me. All my brothers and sisters are still in the area. Two are teachers in public schools. One works at a processing plant. Another works as a clerk at Modesto Junior College. One manages a warehouse-style store in Merced. Another manages a department at a regional restaurant chain. They're all tireless and dedicated workers.

I remember when I was in junior high going to school semi-sick. I didn't think anything of it. It was a matter of this is what I had to do so I did it. No one ever complained in my family. We just worked hard and did whatever it took to achieve success.

Then too, the customer service I offer, no matter what the circumstances, is part of why a lot of past clients keep coming back or refer business to me.

Chapter Eight

Surround Yourself
with Winners

People rise to the level of those with whom they surround themselves. As parents we understand how important it is to influence the selection of our children's playmates when they're small. We're concerned about who their friends are when they're adolescents. I don't know how many times we hear the parent of a troubled kid say, "Johnny just got in with the wrong crowd."

Why do we think things are any different when we're adults?

Those who surround themselves in their professional and personal lives with people who are positive, energetic, honest and vibrant will benefit from those relationships. They will do better and go further. Those who surround themselves with negative people will find it difficult to be unaffected by their presence. Negative mental states are contagious just like the flu or the common cold.

Since so much of what we do in real estate depends on mental attitude, it is critically important for people in our profession to be discerning about the type of people we choose to associate with.

It is possible to learn a lot from observation. As a real estate broker, I have discovered the business health of my organization is significantly enhanced if from time to time very negative people are weeded out, despite the fact they may appear to be productive. No matter how productive they may seem, negative mental attitudes are destructive to those around them—and to the organization as a whole.

The first conscious step for a real estate agent in creating the best environment in which to work—and in surrounding himself or herself with good people—is selection of a broker. It is crucial to find a broker who recognizes real estate agents as valuable customers, treats them with respect and provides them with a good working environment. It is in that environment where agents conduct their professional practice.

A good place to work also means offering a stimulating learning environment. All professionals, whether they are brand new to the business or seasoned veterans, need to be constantly sharpening their skills.

At PMZ Real Estate we are committed to establishing and maintaining those skills through PMZ University, which has comprehensive in-house learning and training centers. There are physical places at our facilities and a curriculum with complete orientation for new agents and ongoing training for all agents, available at no cost, every day of the week.

We also conduct stimulating—though not overly long and burdensome—staff meetings with topical educational content.

A broker, through his or her leadership, provides a tone for the office and the company. At some brokerage firms, agents feel they are treated as children or as employees who are ordered about. This can be very demoralizing to people who have made a conscious decision to enter a profession where they believe they will be in charge of their own destinies.

At some companies management creates a "we" and "they" attitude between agents and the administrative support staff. For instance, clerical staff should be there to serve the agents and provide them with valuable services. But at some firms they work grudgingly, treating agents with disdain or disrespect; they view agents as a nuisance rather than as their customers.

Too often agents will initially make the decision about choosing a broker strictly on who is willing to pay them more. They don't understand that the real distinguishing feature between brokers isn't their compensation plans but the quality of the working environment they offer. That has everything to do with how the agents perform.

If agents walk into a company where there are negative office politics, infighting and backbiting, those things will all inhibit performance. If there is a healthy environment where colleagues who are positive surround agents, and people are upbeat and happy where they work, that will stimulate agents to build successful practices.

In my experience, it is rare to see an agent move from one company to another strictly over money. Frequently people move because they don't feel respected or treated with dignity.

By contrast, my commitment as a broker is based on the notion that agents are among my most valued customers. My entire organization is geared to meeting the needs of agents so they can be free to achieve their goals and objectives.

Agents who are new to the business would be well served to interview a number of agents who work for or were once associated with any broker they are considering. They should find out as much as they can about that company because there are real differences between brokers.

Like a broker, a real estate agent has the responsibility to create his or her own dynamic team. Every agent works with a number of people in related fields. For example, there are escrow officers working with title companies and loan officers who work with mortgage firms. Sometimes clients choose their loan or escrow officers. But agents can have a lot to say about whom to select. It is important to use good judgment in choosing highly talented and responsive people for these roles.

A loan or escrow officer who doesn't know what he or she is doing can kill a transaction. Regardless of how good the real estate agent is, if the deal falls through, it is the agent who will be blamed and the client who will be dissatisfied.

Frequently agents pick loan officers or escrow companies based on a superficial assessment of their capabilities. A loan officer, for example, might be friendly and take them out to lunch, but that doesn't mean they will provide a high quality of service. Agents need to talk with others in the industry and obtain information from as many respected professionals about who is honest, skilled and diligent.

Transaction coordinators are persons who assist agents and their clients by coordinating activities during the escrow process. Agents also will hire assistants to work with them in handling the hundreds and thousands of details that need attention.

If there is one area where many agents fall down, it is in not being critical enough in forming a reliable team that can include a loan officer, escrow assistant and transaction coordinator. Agents must be selective and careful in making sure their teams share their sense of ethics, hard work, responsibility, sensitivity and responsiveness to the client.

PMZ Real Estate is a family business founded by my father, Paul M. Zagaris, who started his real estate career in 1947. Before coming west he was a coal miner in Wyoming and a U.S. Army soldier in World War II.

All four of his children eventually joined him in the business. Today it is run by my sister, Paula, my brother, Jon, and myself. Our brother Steve passed away in 2000.

In addition, my brother-in-law, Duke Leffler, works at PMZ and heads up our Commercial Brokerage Division. Now some from the next generation, our children, are also starting in the business. At PMZ we have a deeply felt conviction that families working together comprise a great business model. This is why we encourage agents to bring family members into their teams.

Real estate offers a unique opportunity for families that want to be self-employed to enjoy substantial financial rewards without being obligated to come up with a large capital investment. For example, if you wish to open a retail store, it requires buying or leasing the building, investing in equipment and furniture, purchasing inventory, hiring employees, deducting and forwarding state and federal taxes, and paying for Social Security, workers' compensation and unemployment insurance.

As real estate professionals, family members get the chance to be compensated well without having to endure all the headaches.

What's more, a genuine synergy can be realized when the people working together are closely related. Everyone contributes to the same pot. The benefits of a practice flow into one family unit and can more easily be shared among the parties without the kind of disputes that can arise when people are unrelated and one person feels he or she is contributing more than someone else.

There is nothing more powerful than a family working together in real estate. My family has worked together and I understand the value of these special relationships. So at PMZ we encourage the participation of people in our company who wish to work with family members.

There are all kinds of different arrangements between families working in this business. At PMZ we have married couples working together, each a strong agent with his or her own book of business—and they cover for each other when necessary. There are couples where one spouse provides support for the other who is more dominant. There are women who take the lead and are backed up by their husbands—and vice versa. There are teams where one spouse's strengths compensate for the weaknesses of the other—and vice versa.

I have seen it a lot and I love it. It is an amazing thing to watch—and it is a trend in our industry.

An individual agent can perform well and build a financially rewarding practice. But at the end of the day a business principally based on personal relationships is not something that can be easily sold to someone else. Clients won't necessarily work with a new agent just because the old agent says so. However, if a son or daughter joins the practice, for example, the agent over time can transfer the relationships that were built up to the child. It is a way to preserve a valuable asset that would otherwise be difficult or impossible to pass on from one generation to the next.

Say an agent who has worked hard over a number of years to establish a lucrative practice wants to start slowing down. The son or daughter can begin covering for the father or mother. The child can come to know and be trusted by the clients. Some day the child can inherit the entire client base from the parent.

Following are a sampling of PMZ agents with stories that supply some examples to consider.

$\sim$

BEN BALSBAUGH
'Inspired by his brother'
(For more on Ben, read Chapters Seven, Nine and Ten.)

I was born in 1973 in Dallas, Oregon. My dad was an entrepreneur. He worked for a garage door company and then owned his own company that builds and installs security gates for residential and commercial properties. My mom is a homemaker who helps with the business.

My parents moved to the Central Valley, to Modesto, when I was very young. I grew up in Escalon, on a couple of acres of almond orchard. I attended Modesto Christian High School with Paul Harmon, another top performer at PMZ.

My parents had four kids. I'm the oldest. My interest was sports. I played football and baseball. My brother Jacob was also very active in sports.

Willy, my younger brother, was born with Kearns-Sayre, a debilitating neurological disease. Sometimes Willy would be the batboy in Little League. He was wheelchair bound for 25 years and passed away in 2009. My mom and sister constantly cared for him. But he was the happiest kid on the face of the planet.

He could never participate. Yet everyone loved Willy. He talked your ear off and was always smiling—even though he was in the wheelchair and couldn't take part.

Willy was always fully aware of his situation. He had dreams: He wanted to be married and have a family. But he would never have them. Life expectancy for someone with his condition was in the mid-20s. But Willy lived to 34 because of the excellent care he received.

So when I have a bad day or I'm struggling with something in my life or something bad happens to me, I think about Willy. I think about him being in that wheelchair every day, not being able to feed himself or do things for himself. And he's happy. That gives you a wake-up call.

In life, people are stuck in this circle of their mind with all this negativity. Growing up with Willy and witnessing him and his spirit allowed me to always keep moving in a positive manner. If he could be happy, good grief, I thought, anyone can be happy. You have to just grab life by the horns—and go.

Willy's life was inspirational. Forget business. Forget career. Forget finances. His life was inspirational.

~

DENNIS LILLY
'A Synergy For Success'

(Dennis works with his wife, Nancy, plus his sons, Zach and Jarod, his sister, Lona Lilly Davis, and lifetime friend and business associate, Derek Wood.)

I was born in Oakdale in 1955 and grew up in Modesto. My

mother was a homemaker. My father worked three jobs at the same time: elected county clerk of Stanislaus County, accountant for Sears and manager of a music band.

After Downey High School I attended Modesto Junior College. I met my wife at age 16. As soon as I graduated from the junior college I joined the Army and got married—all at 19. I went to college at night while I was in the Army and stationed at Ford Ord. While in the service I had a small house-painting and janitorial business. I graduated with a B.S. degree in organizational management from the University of San Francisco after I returned to Modesto to raise a family. My wife, Nancy, obtained her nursing degree at the same time.

I always enjoyed retail sales, having taken courses in high school. I always liked selling services and continued house painting and janitorial management after moving to Modesto on my days off while working for Rainbow Bakery.

I drove a truck for 10 years, selling bread products around the county. There were great people in that business but miserable working conditions, with days going more than 12 hours.

In 1987, I started taking classes in real estate principles and got my license in 1988. I worked part time in real estate sales and then retired from the truck driving route sales job and went to work full time in real estate starting in 1989.

I started in residential and ranch sales at Prudential California Realty. I did really well. I was rookie of the year at the company and among the top in sales six or seven out of the ten or eleven years I was there. I brought my wife in to work with me as my assistant eight years ago. She got her license and we became a team.

We left for PMZ in 1998. The broker I was with was a wonderful guy with a good vision. But his company was slow in moving towards his annual goals. Nothing was really happening as projected.

I watched Mike Zagaris on the other hand establish a good three-, four- and five-year plan on where he wanted to go—and he was accomplishing it.

Mike talked with us for about six weeks before we made the move. My wife, Nancy, Derek Wood (another agent who grew up with me), our lender, Mary Niles, and I all moved together to PMZ and we continue to work as a team.

At PMZ, we initially lost some business from clients who could no longer find us. Eventually we got the business back with hard work and smart marketing. We were doing about $11 million at Prudential when we left. At PMZ, we've been at $27 million to $30 million the last three years. We've been among the top three agents at the company three out of the last six years in volume of units and dollar closings.

Last year I brought in my sister, Lona Lilly Davis, as an agent to assist us with our sales and clients. Also joining us as an agent is our son Zach, who graduated from Sacramento State with a degree in business and a minor in real estate. Now we have five agents plus Mary the lender. We call ourselves the Lilly Group.

The business model we follow is how the Zagaris family has worked together to build a wonderful company, highly recognized in the real estate industry. As a family we've always worked hard and stayed in close contact. Because of our growth and success, other family members have become attracted to the business. My son loves working together as a family in a real estate career.

As a nurse, my wife Nancy definitely knows how to multi-task. She makes a great office manager, assisting with listing management, coordinating transactions through escrow and now acting as our team coach. This increases our ability to close escrows—and to make sure they do close. We have a very low escrow fallout rate; very few of our deals ever fall out of escrow.

Our level of synergy comes from the excitement and fun of working together, being creative, bouncing ideas off each other, exploring different techniques of marketing—and deciding which are more effective for our clients. Up to 42 people can touch a single escrow in some way. When a crisis happens, we decide how to correct the problem—and what can be done to make the process smoother and more effective.

Because of our known ability to close escrows, agents we work with are more receptive to accepting our clients' offers because they know we have a reputation for closing escrows and making things happen so there's a win-win-win-win situation for the buyer, the seller, the buyer's agent and the listing agent.

Someone is always available for our clients. If one of us is out of town, someone else is there to help. Our clients never feel abandoned. They rely on us for information and to get results. When the client runs into problems, especially during the negotiating and escrow process, an agent can't all of a sudden be missing. Everything is built on timeliness and service.

In today's market, we're lacking on inventory. Agents have to be constantly aware of properties that are coming on the market. Instead of one agent looking around for properties or buyers, we have two, three or four agents looking. If one of us sees a property that is suddenly available and might fit the needs of one of our clients, that person brings it up right away. Then we have a greater chance of getting an offer accepted before multiple offers hit the table.

We try to build a reputation so people know we're available to our clients and also to other agents in the transaction as well as the escrow officers, lenders and inspectors. Everyone else in the transaction has to be taken care of. So we need to make sure our clients' needs and everyone else's needs are being met. That's important to us.

All this produces a great environment and a synergy for success in the transaction and for future transactions, too. We get a lot of respect and referrals from past clients. It's not just about us; it's about meeting the needs of our clients and colleagues in the business.

I have found myself gravitating towards successful people I've met—from teachers, coaches and military personnel to current colleagues—because they've been there and experienced both success and failure. Those who succeed come out of setbacks with the attitude that they've learned lessons.

Mike has had many great successes—and a few failures from the past that he is more than willing to share with you. He's the kind of guy who bounces back, constantly thinks of new things and makes them work. He's a pure joy to talk with and be around to explore new possibilities on how both agents and the company can market themselves. He loves to hear and embrace new ideas.

Because he sees his agents as his clients and he very much wants his agents to be successful, Mike gives us the tools we need to sell and be productive. He counsels us on life insurance, personal financing, budgeting—however he might be able to help us benefit from his knowledge and experience. He will talk individually with each and every one of us at the company.

The tools he provides so we can be successful in taking care of our clients range anywhere from state-of-the-art Internet features to quality advertising and signage to well-trained and service-oriented staff. There are great classes continuously offered at PMZ University. He encourages successful agents to teach the newer agents about everything from how to conduct a successful open house to time management to how to handle floor calls (people calling into the office for information on a property) to how to handle questions and answers during a presentation (I've given some of those classes before).

A number of brokers throughout the industry say they treat agents like clients so they can better take care of their clients. But Mike adheres to that commitment to the max. He has never wavered from it. That's one reason why I work with this company. I also like the way the Zagaris family operates. If they say they're going to do something, they do it. They do it well. And they're there for you.

I've been at companies where the staff is good but not up to the level of quality you would expect at a multi-million dollar company. At PMZ, agents really depend on the staff's reliability and commitment at a level of energy that is professional. PMZ has a great staff that has been around, understands the process and assists the agents above and beyond.

In choosing ancillary personnel, you need people with in-depth knowledge who understand that service to clients is king. The lender I use has been in the business for 25 years. She has owned her own company and has managed different mortgage firms. She has a can-do attitude that matches mine. We have not failed any buyer. She pre-qualifies buyers and takes them through the end of escrow. She knows where to take loans to get what buyers would like to have. She acts like the offensive coordinator of a professional football team. It's great to watch her in action.

When you call up and talk with an escrow officer about a client, you need that person to have knowledge of the escrow and its timing even though it is one of many escrows the officer is handling at that time. There are many escrow officers in this community. The ones I use are on top of items in escrow all the time. They are very professional and service oriented with an emphasis on the needs of the client. And management solidly backs them up.

By the way, our youngest son, Jarod, graduated from UC Berkeley with a degree in political science. He has been working for a title company for the past three years in Berkeley and is now full time in Modesto. Jarod is now going to be managing our property acquisition company with my son Zach as part of the Lilly Group. We will always have a bias towards working together as a family.

~

CHRIS SHAW
'Treating agents like customers'
(For more of Chris Shaw's story see Chapter Seven.)

When Mike Zagaris talks about treating the Realtors as customers, that is a very unique attitude—and practice. Most brokers look at agents as quasi-employees, there to provide income to the company.

Mike looks at us as if we are his customers, just as our buyers and sellers are our customers. So in essence, he serves us. Other brokerage companies provide services to agents to assure the companies' success. There is a subtle but important difference. I didn't perceive it initially. Then, after a period of time with PMZ, I saw changes being made. We were already the number one real estate company, yet additional services were being provided to the Realtors®. I realized how important it is to Mike to serve us.

For instance, senior agents, including Mike, provide some of the training. He taps agents in the company with particular expertise in certain areas and invites them to share their knowledge with other agents. It's really a good situation when you can actually learn from other people in the company who are more successful than you are and who are right there in the trenches next to you being exposed to the same conditions.

One of the gripes I have with professional real estate trainers is they talk about how things are in the Midwest, Florida or Los Angeles. That doesn't really have much bearing on what I do here. If I can learn from an agent right here doing exactly what I'm doing who is more experienced and successful than I am, that's extremely valuable and very relevant.

I have had an assistant and a transaction coordinator for about three years. I look for people who are positive thinkers and possess skills that are not my strengths. For example, my assistant is strong with computers where I'm not. My transaction coordinator is very detail oriented, thorough and even-tempered. Since I've hired these people and joined forces with them, my income has gone way up, mostly due to two reasons: They free me up to focus on what I do best, which is to list and sell. And both of these people are more skilled at what they do that I was when I attempted to handle those tasks on my own.

I also used to find it very frustrating to work on the tasks they now handle, especially the escrow process that the transaction coordinator does. I used to work hard all morning on a particularly difficult escrow and then have to hop in my car and try to be in a good frame of mind when I was trying to list or sell in the afternoon. It was tough to be on top of my game.

Now the instructions to my staff are for them to handle the problems until they hit a roadblock, and then bring it to me. They're able to handle most things. It's definitely money well spent if you have the right people.

It's the same thing when you work with a lender. The lender can make your life much simpler by working only with qualified prospective buyers. When they're representing buyers, young agents will work with people who can't afford to purchase or who want to purchase what they can't afford. A good lender will quickly screen out those who won't qualify.

~

ROXANNE BAZUIK
'A little healthy competition'
(Learn more from Roxanne in Chapters Three, Six and Nine.)

I'm a native of Modesto and was born in 1959. My mom worked part time at a clothing store, which was wonderful for me as a little girl growing up. I always had nice clothes. My dad worked for the county as an engineer and road inspector, and then for many years as a painting contractor.

My dad also worked for Paul Zagaris, Mike Zagaris' dad, in the early '70s, doing painting at a lot of his custom houses and custom cabinetwork at his housing projects. So the Zagaris name has been a part of our family for a long time.

I grew up in Modesto, attending Davis High School. I always wanted to be an airline stewardess. I still like traveling. My first job, at age 15 and a half, was at a hamburger joint, Meal on a Bun. I wanted something significant to put on a resume. So I did that for exactly one year. After that there were a series of odd jobs. I worked for a shoe store, which I didn't like, to make money. I was always eager to earn my own money.

After graduating high school in 1978, I went to Colorado with a girl friend. We were young kids who wanted to do a bit of traveling. We had barely any money but got jobs in the Marriott Hotel at Stapleton International Airport in Denver, doing food service for all the airlines. I did that for three years, got married and had a child.

I worked for a couple of years as a receptionist for a real estate company, handling data entry—entering all new business into the computer. Then I got into property management as a leasing consultant in the Denver area. My job was to talk with people as they came through the door about our pricing, show properties and get them into a contract. I was a top producer and made really good money.

In 1991, after getting divorced, I returned to my roots in Modesto, got a job in a leasing office as a consultant for an apartment community and soon became manager, working there for 20 years.

That's where I met my husband, Mike Bazuik. We were married in 1993. We each had a child from our previous marriages and then we had one together.

Mike was in construction then, working for a sheet metal company he owned and still owns.

I felt at a dead end where I was working. I needed some change. So in 2005 I decided to join forces with my husband, who had already gone into real estate, which I had an interest in too. I got my license in 2004.

Working together with my husband was a great opportunity because he was doing extremely well and enjoying it, too. He was already working for PMZ out of its Manteca office.

We're still in Manteca. He is the leader of our pack. He's the motivator. I contribute my great personality. I think I have a great work ethic, even if I don't come into the office at 6 a.m., like Mike does.

We do quite well. We also compete against each other even though we work as a team. We'll say, for instance, let's set a goal: Over three months, between March 23 and June 23, we're going to see who gets the most listings and closed properties. Whoever wins buys the other one a vacation to the place of his or her choice.

I've only beaten Mike once.

Chapter Nine

Achieving Financial Security and a Balanced Life

Although real estate brokers are interested in their agents' performance, few provide agents with wise counsel with respect to creating long-term financial security and achieving a balanced life.

Even though many people in our industry enjoy good incomes, too many of them don't adequately plan for their financial future and end up without economic security when they age. And although many people who come into the real estate business are successful, they end up discovering that the intensity of the career undermines their personal relationships and draws them away from taking proper care of themselves.

Some agents who do well go broke or face serious health problems. That's why planning for financial and personal success is so important. It is why helping agents achieve these goals is an intrinsic part of the PMZ Way. Not only should agents concentrate on being successful in their practices, they need to do it in a way that helps them build wealth and is healthy for themselves and for those around them.

Employees of many modern organizations benefit from a structured environment in which the entity for which they work provides them with the essentials of life, including health coverage and pensions or profit sharing programs. Although income for most of these workers may not be nearly as high as what real estate agents can earn, at least toward the end of the day, when employees are nearing retirement, they can theoretically look forward to some measure of financial security engineered by their employers. That's the advantage of being an employee and working for someone else.

It's different with real estate professionals. Along with all the benefits of being self-employed come real responsibilities. Because agents are the CEOs of their own businesses, they are responsible for creating their own financial security.

You can't start acquiring financial security when you are 65 years old. Buying financial security is a current and ongoing obligation and it must be addressed.

With that in mind, there are some fundamental concerns agents should consistently keep in mind during the years they practice.

• As soon as you receive a commission check, you should immediately put away adequate funds to pay your state and federal income and Social Security taxes on a timely basis. No agent wants to approach the end of the year confronting unpaid tax bills because he or she has spent all of their income.

• As soon as you start in the business, you need to create a tax-deferred retirement account. Most real estate professionals set up a SEP-IRA, or self-employed persons individual retirement account. Again, agents should fund this account out of every single closing commission they receive. Doing so also provides substantial tax benefits by reducing agents' gross income dollar for dollar by the amount of money they contribute to their plans.

• You should set aside money for savings over and above funds earmarked for the tax-deferred retirement account to accommodate long-term family needs. They can range from purchasing a home and financing your children's college education to investing in real estate or other pursuits.

• The best way to accomplish these goals is establishing a personal or family budget. It should include normal day-to-day living expenses—car payments, rent or mortgage payments—as well as contributions to retirement plans and savings.

• These budgets are essential because they help agents and their families live within their means and enable them to invest and save. We live in a very materialistic society. People are inundated on a daily basis with solicitations to consume, spend money and go into debt—especially with the ready availability of credit.

Many professionals in our field get caught up in this material world and spend too much on things they don't really need. Too frequently they end up in vulnerable financial predicaments even though they earn good incomes.

I've known agents making $250,000 a year who have filed for bankruptcy. That can be avoided with a disciplined, intelligent and mature strategy to plan your life.

• Every agent should have a will. When I ask a room full of real estate professionals how many have had wills drawn up, only small percentages raise their hands. Yet having a will is critically important for everyone, particularly for those with small children or substantial net worth. Otherwise, the government will decide what happens to your estate.

• It goes without saying that people in our line of work should own a home. We're in the real estate business. Buying a home is one of the most important investments we can make. And although we certainly may want to refinance from time to time if interest rates drop, it's important to resist the temptation to pull equity out of the house. There is nothing more satisfying than having the residence paid off in full by the time you are 60 or 65 years old. That move can dramatically enhance a family's financial security.

• You should consider purchasing an adequate amount of term life insurance. It is the cheapest form of insurance. You die, it pays. Life insurance should be bought in sufficient volume to cover the needs of those you could leave behind.

I know young agents who are the primary breadwinners in their families and make $150,000 annually. A spouse who works might be earning an additional $30,000 a year. They have three small children, a home mortgage, the usual assortment of bills—and no life insurance. For a very modest price, an agent in this circumstance can buy $2 million worth of term life coverage and know that if anything happens to him or her, the children and the spouse will be well taken care of.

• You also need to take care of yourself physically. There is no question that performing in real estate at a high level involves no small degree of stress. Being physically fit and having good eating habits is critical to maintaining that high level of performance.

Many of the most productive agents are involved in some kind of regular exercise program and are very conscious of their diets.

What's the point of being financially successful if it can't be enjoyed because you end up contracting maladies such as diabetes or heart disease? Many of these health problems can be avoided or minimized with a proper exercise and diet regimen.

• It is also extremely important to strike a balance in your life that involves embracing family and friends. While preparing your weekly plan, purposely set aside time for the significant others in your life. These times should be respected.

This kind of planning is necessary because real estate is not a nine-to-five occupation. If agents don't set aside time to spend with spouses, children and friends, they too often never find the time to do it and end up alienated from those who were closest to them. They may achieve material success, but they end up with no friends or family around with whom to share it. I've seen it happen.

Here are just a few stories from PMZ agents I admire who have made a success out of both their professional and personal lives.

⌒

TIM RHODE
'Striving for balance'
(Read more of Tim's insights in Chapters Six and Eleven.)

For me, taking care of yourself financially and personally is like living within life's wheel—you have to strive for balance. If your career is going well, but you're not putting away for your financial future, your wheel's off track. If you're in a bad marriage or you're having trouble with the kids and things are not as they should be, it's awfully hard to get up in the morning and be the best sales person and human being you can be. Your whole life needs to be in kilter, like the spokes of a wheel.

These are the areas of balance: career, finances, health and fitness, relationships with family and friends, spiritual life and fun and recreation. You have to pay attention to all areas. I had success in real estate, but my life was out of balance. My health habits were bad.

What's often the case with Realtors® is their careers are going great, they are gung ho, but they let some of the other areas of balance fall by the wayside. Neglecting them catches up to you. It's not good for long-term success in your business life either.

For me, the key is stepping outside the everyday business reality— listing or selling a house or solving an escrow problem, the day-to-day stuff—and being able to plan for your future. For me it's all about dreaming. When I'm out getting my physical fitness—usually out in the boonies doing something that is good for my body and mind—I'm thinking about where I want to be one, two, five, ten years from now. It's something people don't do enough of: dreaming, scheming and thinking how I can solve the problems that are in front of me today—and connecting today's dots with where I'm going in the future. I call it big picture dreaming.

There are two sides to achieving financial security: offense and defense.

Offense is the money you make. Defense is living within your means and investing the rest to provide for your future.

Living beneath your means involves, first, knowing what your expenses are. Most people just spend. I know an agent who makes $950,000 a year gross but spends somewhere between $800,000 and $1 million to make the $950,000. She isn't sure just how much.

That's ridiculous. You have to know what it costs you to live.

I'm not talking about living a life of poverty, because most Realtors® make good money. But they spend too much on what it takes to run their business and then they don't take their money and put it in places that will lead to financial security.

The problem I see with most agents on offense is they go through the real estate yo-yo. They have a couple of good months and then slack off a bit. They go on vacation or spend the money or quit prospecting. Then they react with, "Oh, I've got to go to work again." It's like a roller coaster. Their income isn't steady and they never get ahead.

Mike Zagaris has the solution. He says, "Have a plan and work your plan." It is the most simple, brilliant statement I've ever heard him make. But it's so hard to do because it entails what most people don't want to do, which is prospecting.

Prospecting is difficult. People fear rejection. And it's mundane work. But it is the single most important thing an agent can do if he or she wants to be successful in real estate and achieve financial security.

Defense involves living beneath your means, making extra money to take and aggressively invest in what you know best. It is different for different people.

I would see a property I wanted and thought was a good buy in the late 1980s and early '90s. So I'd write a 60- or 90-day escrow and then go out and make extra money just to buy that property. Now I'm 45 and financially independent, basically done.

Two things are extremely important. First, having a long-term financial plan in writing with monthly and yearly goals, which include what you're going to make.

Second, and this is an absolute must, is knowing your expenses—having a profit and loss statement you can see and study. You're in business. We're self-employed people, but most people don't look at their business like a business.

The plan is the goal. The profit and loss statement is the reality. When you see yourself making extra money, putting it in some form of investment and watching it compound, that is magnificent.

For me, putting money in something I know in my local area meant real estate. I knew that type of investment and it was ancillary to what I do every day.

Another thing I do is read a lot of great books, including *The Richest Man in Babylon* by George S. Clason. It's about a wealthy lender back in ancient Babylon and how he went from slave to the wealthiest lender of his day as well as a teacher. It contains simple principles that are priceless. You can also learn about playing defense from reading the book *The Millionaire Next Door* by Stanley and Danko.

In addition, I get together with my accountant and we play "Cash Flow," a board game like Monopoly, but so much more in depth in offering help on how to achieve financial security. We learn from it. The whole idea of the game is how to get out of the rat race and onto the fast track. The game's creator is Robert Kiosaki, who also wrote the book, *Rich Dad, Poor Dad*.

My wife, Tina, and I had been buying mostly single-family homes. When we started playing this game and reading books, we began buying multiple unit rental properties and some commercial property that provide cash flow so at some point our monthly expenses are overtaken by the amount of money coming every month from passive income—income that arrives without having to work for it.

When you arrive at the "fast track," a place in the game, you can go out and do the things you love and dream about even bigger opportunities down the line.

Another issue is personal health. A lot of the top producers in real estate aren't really mentally healthy. They're successful despite themselves because they have so much innate talent. But their success comes from an 'I'll show you' attitude. They are so driven and willing to do whatever it takes to be successful because making money isn't really what drives them; they want to be number one.

I've seen so many people like that. I have been on panels of national experts. They are talented agents but they don't have balance in their lives. Their life's wheel is a little out of kilter.

At one point my wheel was out of kilter too. I was 35 years old, smoking two and a half packs of cigarettes a day, measuring my coffee consumption in pots rather than cups and eating a very unhealthy diet. Ten years ago we started listening to motivational speaker Tony Robbins. I quit smoking and started exercising. I wanted to do more and more things. Last spring, I spent five days in the southern Sierras near the Bishop backcountry, hiking with skis and backpacks. In five days, we climbed five or six 13,000-foot high peaks and skied down them. It was unbelievably physical, lasting from 7:30 a.m. to 7 p.m.

I have run two 26.2-mile marathons. I ran a race 18 miles up Mt. Diablo. I'm an avid snow skier. I love abalone and scuba diving along the North Coast. For abalone, you have to free dive without using air tanks. You go down 15 to 30 feet. I love to mountain bike down pretty wild trails. I'm into any kind of ball sport. I love golf.

I love going out and doing these things. It builds a passion inside me and keeps me physically healthy.

It is extremely important that every part of the wheel is covered. I noticed at one point when analyzing my wheel, friends were low on my personal ratings. So my wife and I intentionally set out to improve this area. We have a group of adult friends we go out with on a biweekly basis. Discovering where your balance is lacking and making a change will go a long way.

Spending time with family goes without saying. I love to have my kids around and spend as much time as possible with them. I'm very proud that in all my years in real estate I never missed a parent-teacher conference or coaching my kids in Little League or boys' and girls' basketball. My daughter did baton twirling. I either coached my children or went to their events all the time they were growing up. This is a great benefit of being self-employed if you make it a priority, which I did.

~

PHIL SCHMIDT
'Always pay yourself first'

(Phil Schmidt has been in the business longer than I. He learned real estate from my father, PMZ Real Estate founder Paul Zagaris. Phil's daughter, PMZ agent Jill Schmidt Parks, learned the business from her father.)

When I first started in the real estate business, I was 23 and had just graduated from college. Mike's dad, Paul Zagaris, hired me. Mike Zagaris wasn't working there yet.

Paul always encouraged people to invest and put money away because there would be pretty lean times given how the real estate market swings. There are peak periods and down periods. During the down times you had better have a nice reserve account in order to sustain yourself, Paul would say. Putting money away takes a lot, though not all, of the pressure off during slow markets because you have the security of your savings accounts and whatever other investments you have made.

I try to tell new agents what's important, like my daughter, Jill Parks, who has been working with me for two years. During that time she has built up a fairly healthy retirement account by putting away the maximum allowed. My accountant is very proud of her. She is only 25 and she will at some point in her life be buying investment properties.

There's an old saying that goes, always pay yourself first.

Paying yourself first means taking the first 10 percent of each paycheck and putting it away. Then you make ends meet with the balance.

When I first entered into real estate, I thought I would live forever. I didn't invest in a retirement account, although I had purchased some income properties. After about 10 years, my CPA, who is one of my best friends, said I had to be putting money away.

Since then I've put in the maximum, about $40,000 every year. It's substantial now. All the young people in real estate need to face the same reality: the market goes up and down and over the long term you will find yourself ahead of the game if you invest and plan for retirement. Plus, the government rewards you through tax benefits for putting money away.

As the end of the year approaches, Mike reminds people that tax season is upon us. "I hope everyone has put money away, at least 10 percent of income, into a retirement account," he says. Mike acknowledges that he can only guide people; it's up to each of us to make the decision. But he highly recommends it and he gives us constant reminders throughout the year.

At the end of each year Mike and our sales manager, Philip Levin, meet individually with each agent to review their goals and objectives for the coming year. They like to see included within everybody's written goals and objectives not only how much money they want to make but what they are going to do with it, including putting money into retirement.

In the middle of the year they review our goals and challenge us: Are we meeting our goals? Are we putting money away? What can they do to assist us?

They always make that offer. These guys care about their agents. Our personal budgets include gas, food, clothing, utilities and mortgage payments. They should also include our investment or retirement accounts, whichever we prefer.

I've been quite disciplined about doing it during the year. In addition, the Zagaris family has been kind in allowing me to invest in some of their properties over time, which has proven very lucrative.

As agents, we're independent contractors, which means we are considered self-employed. Therefore, the government says we will pay quarterly estimated taxes. That means as part of a budget program—in addition to monthly bills and retirement—we need to put one-third of every check away for income taxes, and not touch that money. Again, this doesn't include the 10 percent of income that should be directed into the retirement account.

Setting aside one-third of every paycheck gives us the resources to pay quarterly taxes, including both halves of Social Security.
Another thing an agent has to do is keep a very accurate record of business expenses. A surprising number of people in corporate life don't do that.

In real estate we do have a big overhead. It's important to maintain records because we can deduct legitimate business expenses, but they have to be documented; there has to be a record of them.

What's nice at PMZ is the company keeps very accurate and complete records of all our business expenses, which are substantial— from putting up signs to ordering business cards to postage to long distance business calls to advertising and promotions. The office pays those costs and bills the agent. That makes it very easy come tax time.

It's the agent's responsibility to keep his or her own accurate records on other types of expenses such as cell phones, gas and car payments, and travel and entertainment expenses.

Life insurance is important in our business. As independent contractors, if you're building up a certain amount of wealth, should something happen to you the government will want its share. Life insurance protects family members and the estate so they don't have to draw down investments or liquidate assets to pay estate taxes. Plus, if you're the breadwinner in the family and all of a sudden your income is cut off, the family can be faced with serious financial challenges.

People don't think about these things. They think they're immortal or invincible. But it can happen.

A lot of agents don't have disability insurance. If for some reason you can't do your job by selling real estate, all income can end, but the bills will keep coming in. It's important for people to get disability coverage while they're young and they can qualify for it at cheaper rates.

I don't believe in term insurance. I'm one of those people who bought variable life insurance. It is very expensive when you first take it out, but it can never be taken away from you. It never expires. After a certain number of years you don't even have to pay the premiums; you just keep the insurance. It's like having another mutual fund because the money grows. Plus it's tax-free because it is a life insurance policy. You can also borrow on it for low interest rates if you need to.

What I didn't do, and probably should have done, was plan for my daughters' education. I figured I was making and saving enough money to carry through. What happened was when the children were very young, I bought a few homes, thinking I could sell them to raise the money for college. I ended up financing their college costs using cash flow.

Developing a realistic budget and living beneath your means are sound advice. In the world of real estate, with everyone working on commissions, we have to recognize the market's peaks and valleys. Maybe it was because of how I was raised, but it has always been important for me to put as much money as possible away for a rainy day. So I save a lot of money every year.

People will say, "Phil, you don't need to save. You should be investing the money." But savings is my cushion. After being in this business for 30 years and going through different market swings during each decade—Remember the '80s when interest rates were 20 percent?—I know I made the right decisions. During these times, I often recalled great advice I received from Paul Zagaris: "Live below your means."

We all know people who spend every dime they make. There's a great book I read called *The Millionaire Next Door*, by Thomas J. Stanley and William D. Danko. It shows the contrast between a successful physician who makes a lot of money and the guy next door who has a salary job, but who has budgeted, invested and done all the right things financially. The doctor buys the boat, the second house, the new Mercedes and the country club membership. But when all is said and done, the millionaire is the guy living next door to him.

The message from this book is that overt demonstrations of material wealth are not anywhere as important as planning, budgeting and developing real net worth.

Another lesson I learned early in life was about taking care of myself. I was a swimmer and water polo player in high school and college. There were morning workouts at school every day of the week. Each morning at 6:00, I'd practice until 8 before going to my first class. Then we'd work out again in the late afternoon. That's just how it was.

You learn how to develop a discipline because managing time becomes so important. Today, every morning I'm up at 4 a.m., have a cup of coffee and read the newspaper. I'm at the gym at 5, where I do a lightweight workout and at least 45 minutes or an hour of cardio exercise. Then I'm home, where I eat a healthy breakfast and go off to work. I'm usually at the office by 7:30.

My weight loss and fitness program help me deal with stress during the day. It was always instilled in me to keep in top physical condition if I wanted to be a top performer, regardless of what I was doing and whether the challenges were mental or physical.

Real estate can be stressful. Something needs to help us take the edge off. Eating right and exercising regularly are really important, not just for real estate agents but for everybody. When I occasionally miss working out, I don't feel quite as alert as I would otherwise feel.

I also get a great deal of business at the gym. That's not why I go, but you meet a lot of people. It's another way of prospecting. You're around people so long that they'll let you know they want to sell or they know someone who wants to buy and give you the name.

My family has always and will always come first. My daughters were athletes in school, and I can honestly say I never missed attending one of their swim meets or water polo games the whole time they went through high school. I'd put them on my calendar along with all the other appointments.

Before our oldest daughter, Jill, who is now my business partner, went to UC Santa Barbara, she played for a few years at Modesto Junior College. As her team traveled around the state, I never missed one of the games.

Our youngest daughter, Jody, was on the national team and traveled to competitions throughout the U.S., Canada and other countries. I couldn't make it to all of her games, but I did go to all the games that were in the United States.

I did all that while still enjoying a very successful career in real estate. With about 99.9 percent certainty, I can say my clients knew when I was going to spend time with my family and they respected that. I never lost business because I had to go to an event where my children were involved. During those years everyone knew that every Tuesday and Thursday, I was at the water polo game. I still go out of town to visit my daughter who lives in Long Beach.

It's not like I was taking two weeks off to vacation in Italy. I was fulfilling my duty as a father, and people understood and appreciated it. My clients certainly understand because I encourage them to spend quality time with their families too. I have clients in international business who travel a great deal out of country. But when they're home, they are devoted family people and I'm proud of them.

When I was younger, before we had children, I was really involved with boards of directors and serving on committees for worthwhile community groups. I feel fortunate in that I paid my dues early because it's important to give back to the community.

I still give back financially through charitable contributions. It's important to do that.

But during the years when my children were growing up, I rarely attended parties or strictly social functions because it was more important for me to be home with my wife and daughters.

Your kids are with you for such a relatively short period of time. We made the most of it. I have no regrets. They're both doing great, and I'm so proud.

~

JILL SCHMIDT PARKS
'Taking care of yourself'
(For more on Jill's story, take a look at Chapters One and Three.)

I learned from my father about how to deal with clients on something that for most of them represents their biggest financial investment.

Before I got my real estate license, my dad told me, "You can never sell something you have never bought. You need to buy a house. You need to know what people are going through and the emotions they experience with it. How can you help somebody through a process you've never been through?"

My mom was like, "What are you doing to her? She literally cries herself to sleep at night wondering how she's going to afford this house."

But my dad always talked about "good debt and bad debt. Owning a house is the kind of debt that makes you work harder," he said. "You're supporting yourself. You're taking care of yourself." That's what he told me.

I was stressed. I graduated from college less than a year before. Here I am buying a house and going through all the emotions, including fear. You don't have a set income working in real estate. My dad is a very financially responsible person and he instilled the same thing in me. So I'm worried: How am I going to pay for this?

When you get a commission check, the number one thing is you use half of it for monthly expenses and put half into another account to pay your taxes and to provide for savings and retirement. You have to separate your income. If you can't live on half of your income, you can't afford to pay for what you're doing.

They loaned me the money for the down payment as part of my first mortgage on my first house. I quickly paid it back. With a $1,600 monthly mortgage payment, along with taxes and insurance, on a 15-year fixed, that was a lot of money for me—one person with one income. But I did it, while still putting away half of my income.

It taught me to be responsible for money and to work hard. But my parents have always taught me that. It was never just, "Here's your allowance." We always babysat or did something to make money. But this time, with owning my own house there was a practical lesson: You always pay yourself, taking care of your present and future needs by putting a roof over yourself.

I would say my number one problem is having a hard time saying no. So the hardest goal I have trouble achieving is finding the right balance between family and work. Ours is a 24-hour-a-day, seven-day-a-week job. I have a two- and four-year-old, and I'm a working mom. It was different for my dad, who had a wife who was also a teacher.

I have a 5:30 appointment this evening and won't be home until 7 p.m., if I'm lucky. You never know. When you think it's going to be quick, it takes three times as long. I can't complain about it because we have to work.

Sometimes I'm lucky to get the laundry in the dryer late at night. Being a working mom is hard. My husband works too.

I also come from a very athletic background. My parents are diehards at the gym. I'm trying to find the right balance, working out early in the morning or at the end of the day. It's healthy and keeps you healthy. I'm still not as good as my parents or sister, though.

~

VICTOR BARRAZA
'Building wealth from nothing'
(Learn more about Victor's inspiring story in Chapters Three, Four and Seven.)

I've been in real estate for 15 years. More than four decades ago, my dad was a bracero farm worker. I was a year and a half into the business when I bought my first rental property. I was still living at home with my parents.

It seemed as if every year I did one or two personal real estate transactions of some type. Whenever an opportunity came up, I'd figure out a way to buy the property for myself, whether it was in addition to the real estate I already owned or I was trading it for one I already owned.

At the beginning, the down payment for these transactions came from the commissions I earned. Later the properties started producing income that I used to buy more properties.

All the homes I purchased have paid for themselves with the rental income they generated. Rents have covered the mortgage payment, including principal and interest, and property taxes. What I had to come up with was money for the down payments.

I started with a little two-bedroom, one-bath house in west Modesto that I bought for $51,000 back in 1990. Now I own a number of properties, including agricultural farmland and commercial buildings.

I'm amazed by how many agents don't yet own their home. I firmly believe that's one of the first things they need to do so they can, among other benefits, be able to walk the talk. I believe they should own at least a couple of rental properties so they can also walk the talk when they deal with investor clients. Then they'll know what they're talking about out of personal experience, not just theory. If nothing else, the experience would help them to be more successful in their businesses.

For me, when I have extra money in the bank, I tend to become lazy. So I learned a while back not to keep much money in bank accounts. I need to feel a little bit of a pinch to help me stay driven and focused on achieving my business goals. Not keeping much money in checking or savings accounts is an effortless way for me to work harder.

There are so many options for agents when it comes to investing their money. One of the simplest is real estate because we know what happens long term with appreciation. We work in the business so we can easily manage our properties.

The long-term low risk factor for real estate investment is better than other kinds of investment. And it's easier to invest in areas where you have genuine expertise.

Having said all that, I also believe in diversifying investments and not putting all my eggs in one basket. I try to diversify in real estate. I have residential single-family and multi-family properties as well as agricultural and commercial investments.

My gross holdings were about $51,000 when I started 15 years ago by buying one piece of investment property. Now adding up the gross value of all the real estate would come out to nearly $6.2 million. That doesn't include other types of investments I have.

It is a lot easier for people to get motivated to invest in real estate today than when I started because the market is so good now. When I bought that first house the market was still shaky as to whether it was going up or down. I came in during the late '80s and early '90s when the market was very unstable. I didn't know which way it would head. I decided long term you couldn't go wrong in real estate—even if the market didn't seem to support such a conclusion at that point in time. Also, I decided having excess money in the bank wasn't helping my business grow very much because I was getting too comfortable.

Besides real estate there are certainly other investments people can make. But most of them require paying some other person to handle your money for you. You really have no control over what will be done with the funds. Either your stockbroker or the market will decide what is going to happen. If you want to have some control and be able to increase your holdings, you need to become very educated in order to make wise decisions about where to put your money and when to pull it.

For agents, real estate investment doesn't require four, five or six years of college training in order to have a good sense about how the market is performing and where it is heading. You see that for yourself every day.

As the market changes, there are all kinds of different options for investing and financing real estate. One recent trend is for investors to buy real estate with 100 percent financing.

This is an option that was difficult to find years ago. It is easy to find nowadays. There have been a lot of investors purchasing investment property with no equity in the homes. It is a wonderful thing if we know the market will continue to climb for a couple of years. In the last three or four years we have seen investors who buy with 100 percent financing realizing appreciation of more than $100,000 in equity without having put in hardly any money of their own. It's why so many people have caught onto this method.

But they need to be cautious in going that route because if the market goes down even a little bit, which it inevitably will at some point, these investors could find themselves upside down. We just don't know how much higher the market can go.

Some investors are conservative and others are not. Some want to own less property and have a lot of equity in each one. Others want to own a lot of properties with hardly any equity at the beginning. When you spread your wings out far enough, a little bump on the road can knock you down.

I tell some of my clients who immigrated to the United States with limited English skills and formal education that they can make their money grow just like any university graduate by putting it in real estate. It places a lot of people on an equal footing even if they didn't have the advantage of a good education.

I counsel my clients on their options for investing depending on how much money they have available and their risk level. Those options include real estate, savings and checking accounts, CDs, stocks, mutual funds or opening up their own business. It comes down to what is the safest given their plans. If their plans involve long-term gain, we'll usually discover that real estate is the best option.

I've pointed a number of people into real estate. A lot of my clients who are already real estate investors appreciate the fact we can see eye to eye in finding the right kind of property to invest in. We connect pretty well.

For those who are just getting into the business and want to manage their properties themselves, I supply some of the paperwork they need to get them going: rental agreements and applications, and log sheets to track income and expenses. Or if they don't want to manage themselves, I refer them to property management firms that can handle it for them.

~

ROSE MARIE MENDONCA
'Fulfilling a lifelong ambition'

(Real estate led Rose Marie on the road to financial independence. See more from her in Chapter Three.)

I'm a native of Hanford, California, a small town in Kings County, in the west Central Valley. I graduated from high school there. My dad had a little dairy and did some cotton farming. He wasn't real successful. My mother cooked at the local school.

I knew one thing: I didn't want to milk cows or pick cotton. When I was young, we'd always play Monopoly. You'd buy houses or hotels. I didn't think of selling real estate then, but I thought about buying, owning and investing in real estate.

My ambition was to become a secretary or bookkeeper. After graduating high school, I had a job as a manager and bookkeeper in the office of a Buick auto dealership in town. Then I got married and at 21 moved away, to Stockton. My husband had a job on a ranch. We planted some tomatoes and I hoed 25 acres of them by myself. We lived there for a year and moved to Lockeford, California, south of Sacramento. For 25 years, I ran a hay baling business. I also took care of all our rental properties—houses and apartments my husband and I owned.

In the mid-1970s, I had a birthday. They had a deal where you could take a course in real estate for $75 and learn how to get a license. I wanted to learn the mechanics of taking better care of my rentals. Then I started selling real estate by taking listings at a real estate office.

My first full year in the business I was top sales person in town—and I've been almost every year since. I just try to do my very best at everything I take on, whatever it is. In my hay baling business, I knew a lot of people because I baled a lot of hay. I was a leader in high school of the 4-H Club, which helps young people in agriculture develop their leadership skills. I stayed involved for 27 years. My friend and I ran the biggest 4-H Club in California for the kids in Lockeford. There were lots of members and activities.

I knew a lot of local people through 4-H. Not that many actually became real estate customers, but some did. More importantly, they told their families and friends about me, and that generated clients.

Mainly, I just worked hard. I was at the office working by 8 in the morning and worked until 7:30 or even 10 p.m. almost every day, seven days a week. I still do, except I don't usually work until 9 or 10, but I do work every night.

I kept getting calls from all the companies, including PMZ. At the time, I didn't intend to go any other place. I was content where I was. The first time PMZ called, I said I'd talk to them, but I wasn't interested in making any changes and I didn't want people bugging me. But they could call every once in a while and that would be okay—just don't pressure me. They'd call just to say hi for a year or more. And I'd say hi and exchange a couple of words. Then finally they convinced me to talk with Mike Zagaris.

I didn't want to talk with him because I didn't want to move. By then I saw that most Realtors® were struggling really hard. I felt the Zagarises were sound and I wanted someone with a strong background. That's one of the main reasons I went to talk with Mike—and decided to go with PMZ.

But I had a little team working with me. They weren't sure they all wanted to be at PMZ. But once they all had talked with Mike too, they agreed to make the move, which we did in 2008.

Most people have tried to set goals. I never did, not that I didn't need to. In my head, I've always had goals my entire life. My sister said the other day, "You have to be the best at everything." Why? I don't know. Don't ask me.

I always worked hard at everything I did. Every year I try to do better. Every year I do better.

My kids are both in the real estate business. My daughter in Austin invests in real estate. My son, Rick, works here with me in the same office. He's my right arm.

∽

RICHARD HUNDLEY
'Real estate gave him a second life'
(Richard has achieved through diligence and hard work.)

I was born in Charleston, West Virginia, in 1956, the son of a Union Carbide chemical plant worker who worked his way up from an operator and ended up as manager of a storage facility in Louisiana. He died at the early age of 52. My mom now lives in a senior community in Modesto, close to me.

When I was only one year old, they transferred my father to

Redondo Beach, California, where we lived for 12 years. He passed away when I was in the fifth grade. Then I was back in Louisiana for 18 years, where I graduated from high school and attended a year of college. I didn't take it seriously enough.

I found a job at a chemical plant like my dad, worked there for 10 years but didn't like the shift work. Older people at the same plant told me, "Richard, if you're going to get out, get out now before you encumber debt with the wife."

I'd have stayed at the chemical plant if I had been able to advance, but everyone ahead of me was the same age so I was going nowhere fast. With the 12-hour shifts, including nights, it's a proven fact they take years off your life. We'd be reading articles while doing our shift work. My sister convinced me to come to California and get into real estate.

That's what I did in 1986, at the age of 35. It took me a while to get into real estate. I kept taking classes to get a license, dropping out and then taking them again. Back then, I was working all kinds of in-between jobs: radio advertising, selling appliances, working for pest-control companies. I didn't like any of them. I wasn't sure if I liked real estate either. But I finally buckled down, got my license in late 1989, and joined a real estate brokerage firm. My sister ran an office for the firm in the Bay Area and so she knew the company. In the Modesto area, it was one of Mike Zagaris' leading competitors, the No. 2 company in a market where PMZ was still No. 1.

I didn't want to be in the Bay Area where my sister worked. The pace was way too fast and I'm a country boy from Louisiana. I came over to San Jose, and it was overwhelming. The day I drove to Modesto to look around and get a job, at my sister's suggestion, it was 109 degrees. I thought my sister had sent me to hell. But I stayed.

I was with that company in Modesto for two years until I came to PMZ in 1991. I started calling friends at PMZ because I wanted to move over. PMZ at that time already had the highest standards; it was where you wanted to be.

But at the time, PMZ wasn't hiring new agents. They'd wait to see how you worked elsewhere first. I finally got into sales with PMZ for 13 or 14 years and I've been in management for seven years.

Later, after I was at PMZ, I told Mike Zagaris he needed to start a training program so PMZ can hire new agents and train them our way instead of picking them up after they've been trained someplace else. Mike went with it. Now we have PMZ University, what we call the best training in the Central Valley by any real estate company. I do some of the training. So do a lot of our managers and top aides. And Mike conducts training sessions too. So while I've been here we went from not hiring people who hadn't already been in the business to having the best training anywhere for new agents.

The thing about real estate that appeals to most people at the beginning is the unlimited potential to make money. You can also set your own schedule and have flexibility with that. The biggest thing is you're working for yourself. I didn't like working for other people. I have too many of my own ideas.

Even though I work with Mike at PMZ, I have a lot of leeway. I run things the way Mike wants them run, and I totally agree with his methods and philosophy. He and Phil Levin were a big part of my second life as I was growing up again. They taught me how to move up in business and in life.

One of the main things I didn't realize at first when I got into real estate is you don't have a retirement plan from your company. Mike taught me that you have to pay yourself first by having your own retirement plan. You have to take it out of your commission checks before you start spending your money. If you don't pay yourself first, there won't be any money left over. Mike set me up with two retirement funds that I still have going today.

Another thing I learned is balance. In real estate, it is extremely hard to achieve balance because it's not a normal eight-hour-a-day, five-day-a-week job (eight to five with an hour off for lunch). With a traditional job, your boss and your job dominate a lot of your day. You know what to do because they tell you.

In real estate, you can work 20 hours a day or work eight hours and be just as successful, as long as you learn to work smart.

There is more to balance. If you're healthy, you have more energy and can work more productively. The same thing with family life: If you're happy, you can be more productive. If you're able to stay healthy with diet and exercise and be happy with your family life, both will help you attain all the big goals in your life, including your career goals.

~

AARON WEST
'Discipline from exercise is a key to success'
(For more from Aaron West, see Chapter Five.)

The way I built my real estate business was by creating relationships and keeping in touch. I mailed clients or potential clients something every single month. I stopped by and visited. On Mother's Day, I do a mass stop by—taking carnations to all the mothers in my database. I did 150 last year, stopping by to wish each one "Happy Mothers Day," and moving on.

I learned a long time ago from other successful sales people and mentors I've had that professionals consistently do the same thing. With the majority of people in real estate or any sales sector, everybody's trying to look for the newest, latest and greatest thing. I don't do that. Our industry is a people industry. As important as the Internet has become, with a lot of people worried about web sites and blogs, which do have their place, I think at the end of the day very few people are going to buy a house from a computer. It's all about creating relationships and being professional so when the time comes that people are looking for someone to represent them in the biggest purchase most of them make in their lives, you're the first person who comes to mind. And you're the person who comes to mind when one of their family members or friends is thinking of buying or selling a house.

When clients are referring me to their friends, they're putting their reputation on the line. If I do a good job, it reflects well on the person who referred me. I take that trust very seriously. It's not just me doing a job; I'm representing the person who referred me as well.

On a personal note, exercise gives you the discipline that carries you through the rest of the day. The more you do, the easier it becomes. Your business grows because you have that discipline it takes to carry on. Your brain is clearer and you have more energy. I notice the difference in my productivity when I'm not exercising as much during the winter months.

Staying fit is really important to me because I didn't necessarily grow up as an athlete. I started track runs in 2002 and followed up with it. Gradually, just like a business, I built up my endurance to where I'm doing the long-distance triathlons—the Ironman triathlon is a 2.4-mile swim, 112-mile bike and full marathon of 26.2 miles. You do it all in the course of a day. I've been doing half-Ironmans for three years. I signed up for the Ironman Canada in Penticton, British Columbia, about two hours east of Vancouver.

Real estate is such a chaotic, emotionally charged business. Every day you deal with people who are having issues—with not finding a house or finding one and discovering there are things wrong with it or a husband and wife who can't agree on what they're looking for. Part of our job is almost like being a psychiatrist. There's a lot of people- energy involved in real estate. Being able to consistently exercise gives me some quality "me" time. If I'm on a run or bike, there's not all of that outside energy constantly drawing on my time. So the running, biking, swimming and exercise in general allow me some time for introspection.

Not only is my body benefiting from the exercise, it also allows me to pull myself back to that laser focus so when I'm with a client,

I'm all there.

~

SUZANNE ROBINSON
'Getting high from helping people'

*(A highly successful agent, Suzanne Robinson
is motivated by something other than money.)*

My parents and grandparents were all podiatrists, foot doctors, in the Midwest where I was born in Toledo, Ohio in 1942. My grandfather owned a shoe store and movie theater in Ann Harbor, Michigan, and co-invented the football cleat with Spaulding. He used the proceeds to go to podiatry school.

I went all the way through school in Toledo and graduated from the University of Toledo with a B.A. in retailing. My husband, Robert—now of 38 years—lived nearby. A sister-in-law resided in Danville, California and we loved the weather when we came out on vacation. A job opportunity came up in Modesto for my husband, who is a licensed clinical social worker, which we thought would last for five years.

We loved the Central Valley—the people, the climate; it's two hours from everything. We loved raising our son here. Even though we didn't know anyone at first, we came to love and embrace the community.

When our son was seven I thought about going into teaching. We had lost a child and it was as if I wasn't finished with the nurturing part of life. After serving as a teacher's aide for a year, I realized it wasn't what I needed. I wanted a profession where I could follow my heart. Money is good too; you have to work at something where you get paid.

I went into real estate because I thought I would be helping people fulfill their dreams.

When we first moved to this area, we had a Realtor® who after we came to town said, "Here are three homes in your price range that you can afford. You don't negotiate." There was no give and take at all. She essentially told us, "Here are the three. You pay the price. It's the best you can do."

She never asked what we wanted. It was a very narrow approach to the profession.

Since we were just moving to Modesto, I went along. We did choose a home that was OK. After we moved in we found out the house had belonged to the agent's brother-in-law. The neighbors revealed it had remained on the market unsold for more than a year and a half.

We lived there a year and a half and then got out. Because of the appreciation we didn't lose anything.

I thought to myself: Boy, why didn't that Realtor® pay attention? To this day when I see her, I cross my eyes.

I'm a people person. I love helping people. I'm not bashful. I thought through real estate I could have more flexibility with scheduling if I needed it. My husband and son were number one. My profession was number two.

The first few months after I got into the profession, I was absolutely hooked. I loved the constant change. Every day you get to embrace something new. I had the passion. I can truthfully say I love my profession because it is so personally rewarding.

I do like the money, obviously. The profession has been very generous to me. But that is not my main motivation. I get a real high out of helping people solve the puzzle and find their nest. Every home has a feeling. Every home has a special quality.

My dealings with clients come from the heart. All of my clients are referral based because I've been in business for so long. I've sold some people four or five homes. There's the couple that just got married. Then they have their first child and then a second. One couple just sent their children off to college and I'm helping them downsize. You establish real relationships and personal connections with people. They know I've been here for years and I will be here for many more.

I'll talk people into a house as well as talk them out of a property if I feel it's not the right decision. Maybe they shouldn't sell at this time or they'll be too financially stressed if they buy. I express my true feelings because this is a huge investment for most clients and it can be very stressful for some.

If I believe they are getting in way over their heads or the purchase will place too much stress on them or their family, I'll express my opinion.

"Hey, think twice about this," I'll say. "Be cautious."

Oftentimes a client wants to buy a bigger, newer home. I might ask, "Think about it. You'll have to put in new window coverings, a pool or fix up the yard. Those will all be additional expenses. Do you have it in your finances to be able to stretch that far?"

My clientele boasts a wide variety of age groups, a variable buffet of clients, because I've been in the business for 25 years.

A number of clients, noting that the city is growing so fast, have expressed a desire to retire and move to the mountains. I'll advise caution or raise questions. I've seen situations where there are longtime residents who have lived and worked here. What they really want to do is travel. They see the prices of homes going up so high and realize they have a nest egg in their property.

After two of my clients moved to the Sierras, their children and grandchildren were too busy to come up and see them very often. Their older friends and relatives didn't drive up a lot either. These former clients found themselves coming down the hill for shopping and medical needs. They ended up moving back. "Why did we sell our house and go away?" they asked.

Every client is special. Each of them has his or her own story. They're like personal friends. I love my clients, regardless of whether they love me.

People ask why I don't retire. I love what I do. I will slow down, but can't see myself retiring unless I can't remember where I am or can't get around anymore.

I do take time off. My husband and I are into balance. We take care of ourselves, travel and visit family. When we do, I know I'm covered at the office. I have a licensed escrow assistant and a wonderful team at PMZ. There are several seasoned agents I know who help each other and know how the other works. It's a wonderful weave.

That's what I love about Mike Zagaris and the Zagaris family. I don't think you can be associated with a harder working real estate family behind the scenes than the Zagarises. They give back to the community and they give back to their agents. They embrace their profession. They love what they do just as I love what I do. That's why I'm here.

When I started off in real estate I was with a major national franchise company because I thought it would open more doors. I could be behind their name. I found out within the first year that this wasn't the case. You're an independent contractor. Clients come to you for your service.

Whenever I used to represent a client and the other agent was with PMZ, I was always pleased because I knew each of its agents was seasoned, got the job done and I didn't have to do their work for them. They performed their part of the transactions and I would do mine. I was impressed.

Twenty years ago I moved to PMZ. I found out later Mike Zagaris had talked to his staff at one of their morning meetings about how his organization was growing. "If there are any agents you've had escrows with who you'd like to come work at PMZ, let me know," Mike asked. "I'll contact them."

Mike called me.

At the time, PMZ was a male-dominated office. I loved it because the agents dressed for success. All the guys wore suits and ties. (It's somewhat more casual now.) Everyone had a four-door car—a mobile office—that was cleaned, polished and ready go to.

At first when Mike called and said there was room for me at PMZ, I was concerned. I felt I would have to work harder amid more competition; I wondered whether I could step up to the plate and meet his standards.

Mike is a very quiet, but extremely brilliant guy. He embraces all his agents, understanding what we need in order to do our jobs well. Every week Mike has a morning meeting where he often covers the latest happenings in the world and how they affect our marketplace. He constantly encourages us to think in terms of our own personal growth.

I look forward to the morning meeting every week. I wish they would last longer than a half-hour or hour. Mike always listens to what we agents have to say and pays attention. I could listen to him speak for hours. When he addresses groups like the Board of Realtors®, I love to go and hear him.

Shortly after joining the firm, I needed help for one of my clients from PMZ's commercial department. I found a qualified commercial person to help. PMZ is a full-service organization, meaning it's full service for my clients.

They are number one for me. If I have a client whose husband needs to rent commercial space for his business office, I can direct him to many seasoned professionals in our commercial division. If one of my clients wants to buy 100 acres of agricultural land, I have someone who is experienced and can serve him or her at PMZ. If I have clients who are new to town and say they can't yet afford to buy, there is a rental division at PMZ where I can help them get assistance. I can obtain the keys to homes, take them out and show them the rentals.

When I joined PMZ, Mike's father, Paul M. Zagaris, had just passed away. Mike became president of what was renamed PMZ. At that time my husband and I owned a home in a subdivision that was almost paid off. Our accountant said we needed tax write-offs. We shouldn't own a house that was paid for, he said.

Paul Zagaris built many of the popular established subdivisions in Modesto. He developed the lots and sold them to builders. He developed Eastridge, Eastridge Plaza, River Heights, Sherwood Forest and Dutch Hollow, where we now live. PMZ was building homes at the time through a custom home division.

We were looking to buy another re-sale home when I talked with Steve Zagaris, Mike's brother, who was building homes for PMZ. He was extremely talented and had a wonderful eye for architecture. Building a custom home from the ground up with Steve's help benefited me a great deal. I saw the flow of construction, the materials, floor plans, how it was built—everything connected with the home. It gave me a deeper appreciation than you get from selling only re-sale homes.

Steve had volumes of information about home building. He would take my husband and me aside and explain anything we wanted to know. He was always up on the latest technologies and was very interested in making new housing more energy efficient. Steve was always a leader in the building industry. He was always taking the next step and looking ahead into the future. He really paid attention to detail.

It was a great loss when we lost him to cancer in 2000. We will always miss him.

It was very comforting to me to find people like Steve Zagaris within the organization. It was reinforcement that I had made the right decision to be at this firm.

This love of the profession has carried through to all of us who have worked here over the years. You want to help the people at PMZ and be part of this winning team. They've done very well and been very good to me. And I've been very good to them. It's a two-way street.

Taking time for yourself is also important because you need to have a solid base before you can branch out in the world. Every morning my husband and I have breakfast together. We spend time in the morning chatting about our day. If he has to be at the office at 7 a.m., then we talk at 5:30 or 6 a.m. It doesn't matter. You have to pay attention to these things.

We make time for ourselves. We schedule time off with each other just like we're setting other kinds of appointments. That time can fall on a Tuesday or a Thursday. If one of my clients calls on that day, I say I'm on an appointment; I can't speak with them today but I can be with them on Friday or Saturday.

I do work a lot of weekends because that's when many of my clients can be free. My husband understands. If I have to work on a weekend day, he'll go off to work at one of our duplexes or perform yard work at home.

I'm a big Giants fan and we go to baseball games in San Francisco. Or we take the dogs for a walk and turn off the cell phones. You have to do that.

Having balance in your life also means eating right. I could exercise more, but I take walks and make sure I do yoga. If I'm really stressed, I get on my stationary bike on the gazebo in the back yard so I'm not as anxious.

My husband and I always thought we would live off his income and save mine. It helped too when our son went to UCLA, which wasn't cheap.

We want to make sure our home is paid for, which it almost is. The cars are paid off. We have a variety of investments in our portfolio. Yes, I own some real estate properties and some stocks. Our accountant says we need investments.

Some of our properties are paid for. We don't want to have to depend on Social Security. We desire a nice lifestyle where we can live off our dividends and income. We have always saved a minimum of 10 percent of what we earned. In some years it was as high as 20 percent.

When real estate agents embrace this profession they have to embrace the total picture. Too many agents get into this business because they want to make easy money. They are usually the first ones to leave it. Yes, it does pay well. But you also have to work hard at it. You can't be an order-taker. You have to be a giver—as in giving service.

I stress to those agents just getting into the business that they have to save those paychecks because there are taxes to pay and things to do. I've seen a number of new agents make good money and end up not having the funds to pay taxes at the end of the year.

Still, money is not my motivation. What motivates me is having a passion for what I do. It has also served me well financially. But I would do this job for $5 an hour in a heartbeat.

Our whole office will participate in the lottery. The agents always laugh and say if the office wins the lottery everyone will be in the limousine the next day headed to Sacramento, except Suzanne. I'll be in the office, working.

I think when you're free of financial pressures you have the freedom to help your clients. They know you're dealing with them from the heart and not just because you have a car or house payment to make.

My repeat customers know how I feel. Many times I've had clients interested in buying income property they can have for themselves or their children. If I feel it is a sound investment, I encourage them. "If you don't want to buy it, I will," I'll say. "Or if you don't want it in a year or two, I'll buy it back." And I'm serious.

I want my clients to be comfortable financially, have less stress and prepare for retirement too. I'm not a financial planner, but I am careful to ensure my clients feel good about their real estate investments.

Oftentimes I have relocation clients. I handle clients on behalf of some large companies that are bringing new employees to town. I'll pick up the wife, get in the car and visit all the area schools. Schools are important for families with children. They're coming from different parts of the country.

I don't know the special things they need for their children. I do know which schools have the best test scores. But the families need to visit campuses and get a feel for the pulse of the schools and hear the laughter of the students. I realize they each have their own comfort zone. So I sometimes need to take a little more time with my clients to be sure they get it right.

∾

ROSA GONZALEZ
'Staying together'
(For more from Rosa, see Chapters Two, Three and Six.)

We have fun with my five-person team. I remind them at least once a week that, yes, we're here to work and achieve goals. But we're also here to be happy. We can't help other people if we're not laughing and smiling. I enjoy my two assistants very much. I've gotten to know them outside of work and care about what they care about. It makes it so much better at work. They don't just feel like they're working here; they feel special.

My philosophy is to help others. My goal is not just to have employees, but people I can mentor in order for me to give back for what I received.

Both my assistants, Andrew and Brian, in their early 20s, are in the developing stages of their lives. Giving them the opportunities to learn good business practices will catapult them into being successful when they're ready to go out on their own or pursuing other careers, whether they stay in real estate or decide to do something else. What they're learning with me isn't just the day-to-day job. It's learning how to run a business and learning why success comes to you. It's all about giving back.

I've learned that I didn't do enough of that in the days I ran my dad's business. I primarily learned it from the opportunities that my real estate mentor, Jerry Katzakian, gave me.

My husband, Abel, and I go to the gym together a minimum of three times a week. He drives a truck and has set hours. That way we stay healthy and get to spend time together. We also enjoy gong to church together on Sundays and afterwards, as often as possible, taking bike rides, weather permitting.

We make time for each other. When I'm working late, which is every day, he'll either come home with fruit or just hang out with me. He'll read. At least we're in each other's presence. Sometimes I'll take the work home with me after 7 p.m. so we're still together.

<hr />

BEN BALSBAUGH
'Having someone to share with'
(There's more from Ben in Chapters Six, Seven, Eight and Ten.)

I'm at a good place professionally. I was married young, at age 24, for four years. It ended in divorce when I was 28.

I come from a conservative time and place. There was not a lot of divorce in my family. From a personal standpoint, I resisted grasping onto more specific family-oriented goals because I didn't feel worthy of them. Once I forgave myself for mistakes made in the past, during the last five years I've been able to get to a place where I'm healthy enough to set good financial and personal goals. I may not be sure exactly what form those goals will take, but I'm looking forward to what the man upstairs has in store for me.

What happens when you're 85? No matter how successful you are today, if you don't have anyone to share it with, where are you?

I'm single now, which is okay. But there have to be goals beyond making money. I've grown a lot personally over the last five years.

～

ROXANNE BAZUIK
'Finding balance'
(Read more from Roxanne Chapters Three, Six and Eight.)

Work can take up 12 hours a day, six days a week, but with 80 percent of the weekends off now. We try to balance home and work to allow us to retire early and enjoy the fruits of our labors.

I have no problem working hard. I'm a very hard worker, and always have been. Mike, my husband, works very hard too. But we do need to find our balance between work and play. I would love to have a little more playtime. Ultimately, we will reach that point and I hope it's within a 10-year period of time. After that I do want to slow down. I don't want to be working 8 to 16 hours a day. By the time I'm 60, I want to be partially retired.

～

MIKE BAZUIK
'The balancing act'
(Mike has more to say in Chapters Two, Six and Eleven.)

The balancing act is kind of tough in this industry. If I go back several years, when deals were flying in from the banks, the balancing act was easier. I took every Friday off. We'd go to dinner with family and friends Friday nights and spend time with the family on weekends.

Now it's a little bit harder. We still go out on Friday or Saturday nights to hockey games. We do dinners once a month with friends. Of course, Sundays we try to take off, but don't always get to. We bought a lake house at Clear Lake in Lake County. It's 2,200 square feet, right on the water. I converted the upper half of the house—two bedrooms, one bath with a family room and kitchen from a one-time bar area—and we rent it out full time. We have the bottom half: one bedroom, big living and family rooms, dining area and kitchen with a deck and garage. It gives us a place to go and still gets us income to pay off the property.

We make time for family and friends even when the market places greater demands on our time. I may still work mostly seven days a week for three or four weeks, but then deliberately schedule some time off for myself and the family.

~

KAREN SERPA
'Not consumed by work'
(She is also in Chapters Three, Six and Ten.)

It didn't take me long after getting into real estate to realize this business can consume you if you let it.

I used an appointment book. If my daughter had something at school or softball practice, it went right into my appointment book and calendar along with the appointments with my clients.

I try my best to balance my work with my personal life. I don't always accomplish everything I want to do with my personal life, but that is my goal.

Chapter Ten

Give Selflessly

It is my belief that what goes around comes around. Agents who give selflessly of themselves to their community are rewarded with their community's embrace. By giving, agents invariably weave themselves into the fabric of their communities and develop both visibility and reputation. By working alongside like-minded people, others gain a positive sense of an agent's character and personality.

We are blessed to be able to live in our country and participate in the exciting and rewarding business of real estate. The least we can do to express our gratitude for these blessings is to give back to the communities in which we live and work.

At PMZ Real Estate we strongly encourage our agents to get involved in community activities. This involvement is an integral part of the PMZ Way.

Agents often ask me what to get involved in. "Start with what you are interested in," I'll respond. If your interest is athletics, consider coaching a little league or soccer team. If your interest is in helping the less fortunate, get involved with one of the many service clubs or charitable organizations in your community. There is a veritable cornucopia of civic, church, political and neighborhood organizations, projects and causes that sorely need volunteers.

Through acts of giving and caring that are too numerous to recount here, individual PMZ agents represent the best tradition of giving back to their communities. Here are just a few of their stories.

$\sim$

BEN BALSBAUGH
'Growing from community involvement'
(For more from Ben, see Chapters Six, Seven, Eight and Nine.)

Part of being able to grow personally as well as professionally in recent years has been the fact I've always been active in the community.

I'm blessed with a large extended family and a huge sphere of great friends. There's a group of guys I grew up with. All of our parents were friends, too, when we were growing up. We played softball Monday nights during the spring and summer for 17 years. We played poker Monday nights in the winter.

We were all good friends. People tell me I have a lot of best friends.

I'm involved today in an organization called the Central Valley Professional Exchange. It's made up of 20- to 40-year-olds. It's a networking group, almost like a Rotary Club for the younger generation. I'm president. We meet monthly in Modesto—although it reaches throughout the Valley—and hear speakers. They include the city manager, the president of nearby California State University, Stanislaus, and business leaders. We view ourselves as the next generation of leaders—so we bring in and hear from the leaders of today so we can learn from them.

We also put on fundraisers. For instance, we raise money so we can pick up the underprivileged kids at Brett Hart Elementary School and take them to the mall. We spend $150 on each of the kids, buying them school clothes plus odds and ends they need. Then we meet at the local pizza parlor. Santa will turn up with the kids' favorite toys. It's a way to give back.

There is other charitable work. During Thanksgiving and Christmas, I get involved with groups feeding the homeless and serve food at the Salvation Army. I'm always active doing things where I can be a volunteer as opposed to organizing or leading.

I've served as budget advisor for the Big Valley Grace nondenominational church in Modesto, helping members of the congregation plan their finances. A lot of people in the community are struggling. They don't have the tools to budget and live within or beneath their means. I help counsel some of them. I love meeting with young couples who have a kid or two. You get a lot of joy when you see them take the plan you've helped them develop, implement it and see the benefits. Sometimes they save an extra $25 one month and have a great date night out. It goes all the way up to a couple being able to finally save money to buy their own home.

What I most recently found very personally rewarding was participating in the Valley Apprentice campaign. Spearheaded by a very prominent and successful local entrepreneur, Dan Costa, Valley Apprentice was created to benefit four local nonprofit organizations: the Center for Human Services, the Sierra Vista foster care program, the Society for the Handicapped and the Salvation Army's Red Shield Center aiding disadvantaged kids in south Modesto, providing them with a safe and alternative place to go instead of roaming the streets.

Inspired by Donald Trump's "Apprentice" television program, Dan Costa took 100 applicants to be contestants in his own local program called Valley Apprentice. The list was narrowed down to 20 people, including me. We were placed on four teams of five members each, each team assigned to come up with ways to aid one of the four nonprofit beneficiaries. Assignments were made when the director of each nonprofit pulled names out of a hat. I was randomly chosen to serve on the Salvation Army team.

First, my four teammates and I assessed what was most needed at the Salvation Army Red Shield Center. We visited the nonprofit and interviewed the captain of the local Salvation Army. We determined the kids desperately needed a gym renovation and additional programs to offer them more opportunities.

Over the next 10 weeks, our team raised more than $100,000.

It was used to install a brand new gym floor. The funds also went to start two new efforts at the center: a visual arts program where area artists were brought in to teach the kids about painting and a culinary program where local chiefs volunteered their time teaching the kids how to cook.

At the end of the 10 weeks, in July 2011, all four teams gathered before a big crowd for a major event at the Gallo Center for the Arts in Modesto. Each team spent 15 minutes presenting highlights from its project to the crowd and to Don Costa. He also brought to Modesto Eric Trump and Don Trump Jr., Donald Trump's sons, who served as judges in the boardroom-style contest at the Gallo Center.

Each of the four teams raised more than $100,000 to benefit their nonprofit group. In all, more than $750,000 was raised to finance worthy projects for the four organizations.

After the team presentations, an overall team winner was selected. Then each five-person team anonymously voted to designate an MVP for the team. The MVPs were also announced that evening. I was chosen as MVP by my teammates.

The whole Valley Apprentice enterprise was the subject of about 20 articles in the *Modesto Bee* and other local news outlets. It was a big deal.

The following month, as a reward for all of our hard work, Dan Costa flew me and the other three MVPs on his private plane to New York City. We met Donald Trump, had dinner with Eric Trump and visited the floor of the New York Stock Exchange and Ground Zero in lower Manhattan.

Because of my experience growing up with a severely handicapped brother who eventually passed away, I was always interested in helping the handicapped. When I was picked for the Salvation Army team I knew nothing about the Red Shield Center. But in the course of participating in Valley Apprentice, I learned so much about the great work this nonprofit is doing for kids and got to do some neat things for them myself.

It just affirmed what I learned from Mike Zagaris about the importance of giving back to the community.

~

JEANNIE MACDONALD
'Real estate is about people, not money'
*(From a prominent Modesto family, Jeannie MacDonald
learned at an early age about the duty to give back.)*

I was born Modesto in 1945. My father was in the grocery business. At one time he had three stores in Modesto called Angelo's Markets. My mother was a homemaker. After finishing Downey High School, I attended Stephens College in Columbia, Missouri, where I got a degree in sales and marketing.

I went to work for women's clothing stores in California, starting in Modesto and then in Southern California, where I met my husband, Tom MacDonald. His work took him to St. Louis, Missouri, where I worked for clothing stores in the Midwest and eastern seaboard.

After our first child was born, we moved back to Modesto in 1973. Mike Zagaris' father, Paul Zagaris, and my father were very good friends. Paul had offered my husband, Tom, a job. So Tom took the class in real estate, passed the test and went to work for Paul Zagaris selling real estate. I worked in our family's grocery business, mostly purchasing gourmet food and cookware products.

The grocery stores were sold when my father passed away. I came to work with Tom. At the time there was no such thing as assistants and transaction coordinators for real estate agents. I was probably one of the first personal assistants. I handled Tom's marketing and transactions starting in 1988.

By 1990, I had my own license. So in addition to my other duties, I also started selling. Business was great. I've always been very active in the community so it was very easy to market us because people were very familiar with my family's name, Angelo, and the

MacDonald name as well.

The Angelo family philosophy that was passed on to me is that we give back to the community that supports us.

I'm on the board of trustees for Memorial Hospital. I've been involved with Omega Nu, a women's sorority in town that does a lot of fundraising for community projects. I have been on the board of directors for the Center for Human Services, working mostly with children in crisis and providing family counseling. I'm also on the board for the Family Service Agency, a similar type of organization.

Plus I'm very involved in a Realtor®-sponsored community event called Christmas CanTree, which raises money and collects donated food items for the Salvation Army. This event started here in Modesto through the Realtor® community and has spread nationwide.

We do a lot of fundraising in real estate. We raise money for Community Housing and Shelter Services, which gets donations of housing and clothing for the homeless in the community. I've been on the boards of a number of similar groups over the years.

It's part of a family tradition that was instilled in me. There is tremendous self-satisfaction from doing it. It makes me feel good.

Name recognition is very important in real estate. If you're out in the community doing worthwhile things, people come to know you. And they want to do business with people like them. So when it comes time to buy or sell a house, they think, Jeannie and Tom MacDonald are just like us. Why not do business with them?

When you've been active in the community and in business for 30 years, like my husband has, there are a lot of referrals. It's not the reason you get involved in the community, but it's certainly one outcome.

I like to let other people take the glory for the work we do. It's not my thing. I enjoy the job we're doing together. I love what I do.

Real estate also should never be about the money. It should be about the people. It can be about the money, but then you don't get the genuine sense of satisfaction that comes from helping others in need.

What's really fun when you've been in the business these many years is when we sell to second-generation clients. Now the children of previous clients are turning to us when they want to buy and sell real estate.

That's great. It's what you work for. It is the kind of business you want to create over the long term: having people so satisfied with what you do that they repeatedly refer to you and use you for their own personal needs.

~

ERIC INGWERSON
'Making a big difference'
(Eric served for years as a public official in his native Ceres, where he still lives.)

I was born here in Ceres in 1954, and never left. My father was a meat cutter for a while and then part owner and manager of a liquor store in Modesto. My mom was a housewife for many years and also worked at the local drug store.

I graduated from Ceres High School in 1972. I was going to go to Modesto Junior College but was really tired of school. So I was hired at Delta Brands, the Budweiser distributor in Modesto. Back then Budweiser wasn't as popular as it is today so I would be laid off in the winter months when beer sales were slow.

Then I worked for McMahan's furniture store as an assistant on the delivery truck. I was promoted to assistant warehouseman, then head driver on the delivery truck and then head warehouseman. At age 20, I started in furniture sales, working in the warehouse Monday through Friday, and working Saturdays in sales while I learned to sell. I became assistant manager for the McMahan's store in Modesto and later went to work as a salesman for Rice furniture store, also in Modesto.

My uncle, Don Sanders, was a real estate broker. He said there wasn't much of a future in the furniture business. He kept talking to me about getting into real estate. By then I was 25 and married to my high school sweetheart, Carol.

One day a friend, Randy Huggins, a real estate agent who was a couple of years younger than I, came by the furniture store driving a brand new Cadillac El Dorado. It looked like a big boat. "Eric, I just paid cash for this car," he told me. "You've got to get into real estate."

So in 1980, my wife and I borrowed $20,000 by taking out a second mortgage on our house with a 13 percent interest rate and 15 loan points. I didn't have a clue what a loan point was then. The payments were interest-only with a balloon payment due after three years. I was handed a check for $16,800, representing the $20,000 loan less the loan points.

We lived on that money. I quit my job at the furniture store and went to school full time to take the real estate exam, attending classes every day at the former Anthony Real Estate School in Modesto. I took the test and passed it.

I went to work in 1981 for the uncle of Randy Huggins, my friend with the new car. The real estate market had just come off a boom during the late 1970s. I got into it when it hit the skids. The prime interest rate soared to 22 percent that year.

It was very difficult to survive the first two or three years. My wife worked full time as a dental assistant while I sold real estate and worked seven days a week nonstop doing what I could to make a deal. I made $13,000 the first year in business. We were excited with the thought I was making any money at all during that time.

No one wanted to do new financing because the interest rates were so high. We took motorcycles and boats as down payments. Every deal had to be put together with loan assumptions. You could legally assume loans in those days. We would carry a loan to serve as our commission, collecting the money in monthly payments because there wasn't enough cash generated in the transaction to pay the agent. I would sell my notes for 50 cents on the dollar to my own broker in order to raise enough money to pay the monthly bills.

Things became better. Interest rates dropped to 12 percent in 1984, and everyone celebrated. When interest rates came down it made it easier to get loans to buy homes. (Later on they passed a law banning the assumption of loans without qualifying for them.)

I made $40,000 in 1985. I thought to myself, This is living. I went down and bought a new 1986 Chrysler Fifth Avenue, the first time in my life I owned a new car.

The agency I worked with closed down and I went to work for another broker under a national franchise name in 1988. I had no interest in leaving Ceres for a larger office. I worked two blocks from where we lived. Things were going well.

One day in 1994, I got a call at home from Mike Zagaris. I wasn't interested in switching over to PMZ. He persisted. "Give me 20 minutes," Mike said. "If you don't like what I have to say I'll never bother you again."

I drove to Modesto, met with him and after 20 minutes he convinced me to quit where I was at in Ceres and go to work for the Zagarises.

That was the best move I ever made in my real estate career. I've been more successful in my time at PMZ than I ever was at any of the other offices where I worked. I didn't realize what I was missing: the great support staff, the advanced technology, the continuing training for agents and the opportunity for business expansion.

In 1997, PMZ opened an office in Ceres. I was the sales manager for six agents. Now we have 28.

My own business has definitely increased. Before coming to PMZ, in my best year I made $60,000. Every year at PMZ it went up. I earned $100,000 my second year at PMZ. Now I am at more than twice that amount. Overall, it's gone up four-fold.

Much of the credit also goes to community participation.

In 1982, the father of a longtime friend, Jim Cooper, asked me to attend a meeting of the Ceres Lions Club. I didn't know if I wanted to be part of the Lions Club. I considered it a bunch of older guys and didn't think I'd fit in. After first turning down the invitation, I went to a meeting.

Surprisingly, there were younger guys there too. I wasn't at all thinking of joining a service club to enhance my business. At that point I joined the Lions Club thinking I'd stay with it to do my civic duty or help the community for a year or two and then get out.

That was in 1983. By 1989, I was president of the club and I'm still a member.

The Lions Club is a service organization that raises funds for community projects, from Boy Scouts and youth sports to completing improvements at local parks to helping other groups.

During that time, two people—the mayor and my neighbor, Greg Smith, who is also in real estate—asked me to serve on the city of Ceres Planning Commission. Greg said being on the commission would keep me in touch with what is going on and allow me to know where all the new development was going in.

I applied and was appointed by the City Council in 1988. So often people live in the same small town all their life and never have a clue about what's happening around them. By becoming a planning commissioner, I could see where development was going and who was building what and where. Of course, if a matter before the commission had anything to do with the real estate company where I was working, I immediately excused myself to avoid even the appearance of a conflict of interest. That happened only occasionally. Where it helped me to serve was gaining first-hand knowledge of what was happening because I was voting on it.

After seven years on the Planning Commission, I ran and was elected to a seat on the City Council in 1995. I served until 2003. I also served nearly two terms as mayor of Ceres. In addition to elected office, I also served as a member of the board of directors of the Ceres Chamber of Commerce.

Public service was a challenging experience. Being on the council, moreso than the Planning Commission, not only kept me on the cutting edge of growth, but also allowed me to become a policy maker helping to shape the city and community into a better place.

I think I helped make a big difference. During my tenure on the council we grew economically and industrially, expanded the Fire Department, brought in a huge new grocery distributor, created jobs and purchased property where a new community center will be built. We expanded the park system and youth recreation. We renovated the city's rundown baseball complex.

There are negative talkers who like to complain that the City Council has real estate people on it who are in it just to bring in more housing and developers. I was convinced that we needed to grow in Ceres in a positive way. That involved expanding our economic base as well as our housing stock.

All this involvement helped me because everyone knew I was a real estate agent. It opened doors. They'd say, "Eric sells real estate. Let's give him a call." I was introduced to so many people I would never have met otherwise. It created a client base that turned into a big part of my business.

Agents who are new to an area will engage in prospecting. They will often open the phone book and start calling people in the community. It's tough duty. You get a lot of rejection.

I didn't realize it while it was happening, but I was doing my prospecting in Ceres through my meetings and acquaintances made at the Lions Club, the Chamber of Commerce and the City Council.

Now I teach a class for new agents at PMZ University. I ask the students, "How are you going to get your name out to people who don't know you?" Then I ask, "How many of you belong to a service club or a local chamber of commerce?" Not many hands go up.

I then advise, "Join one. Call the chamber. They are always looking for new volunteers. Become involved in your community. Pretty soon people will come to know who you are and what it is you do for a living because you're going to get chances to tell them at various functions and events."

I also tell the new agents that by doing these things, the community will get to know and trust them through activities that don't involve real estate. It certainly helps if clients already know and trust you when they need to be represented in the biggest investment they'll make in their lives: the buying or selling of their home.

~

KAREN SERPA
'Seen as a trusted friend'
(See more from Karen in Chapters Three, Six and Nine.)

I'm very active in the Oakdale community where I live, work and focus my business. I'm a board member of the Oakdale Cowboy Museum. We put on lots of community events and raise money for scholarships. We sponsor a Chamber of Commerce mixer during rodeo week in the springtime.

I am involved in my daughter's parent-teacher club at her school. I'm involved in the Relay for Life, the American Cancer Society event, where you raise money for every mile you walk. I'm involved in a therapeutic horseback-riding group. It gets handicapped people to ride horses as a way to give them more freedom to get around and be active, especially for wheelchair-bound people.

I'm involved in Rotary Club. We have a dinner for about 500 people raising money for the hospital foundation, scholarships—all the things Rotary supports.

One of the things I do is have an ad on the shopping carts at the local grocery stores. I've been doing that for more than 10 years. I can remember only one instance where somebody called me after seeing me on the shopping carts. But I run into people and they say, "Wow, I see your signs everywhere. They don't necessarily since I don't have many of them. What they see is my face—on cards, at community events—and they recognize me. I've found that's a huge tool. When people are thinking about selling their house or maybe one of their kids wants to buy a home, they look for someone they feel they can trust. And with my visibility in all these different ways, people in my community feel like I'm already a friend who can be trusted.

I believe in giving back to the community that gives so much to me. It's also a good business practice because people see that you care about your community and the people who live in it. I think people appreciate that. Also, I make a lot of contacts and there are a lot of networking opportunities. Many of them produce clients.

You can have fun being active and giving back, too. People remember you in positive ways because of it. It's all about letting that passion come out. I love what I do, whether it's work or community involvement.

I've heard lots of motivational speakers over the years. One thing I heard when Jim Rohn spoke really stuck with me. He said to watch what you become in pursuit of what you want. That tells me to continue to be a nice person who cares about people; that it's not all about the dollar—that it's not about what I can get from my clients, but rather what I can do for them.

∾

JOSEPH BONDI
'Opening the door'
(Joseph can also be found in Chapter Three.)

Everybody knows I'm Catholic. It works well for me. You see subtle Catholic things in my office: An eight-inch high statute of Our Lady. A small cross is above the door. They don't overpower.

I help out through the local diocese with a Catholic retreat, Journey in Christianity, to bring people closer to God. I also work with a small nonprofit group called Civitan that provides services to other groups, like supporting the Walk for Life and the Howard Training Center in Modesto.

It's all been very rewarding for me. I never ask for business from the people I meet when I'm doing this work, but they bring it to me. Once they open the door to conversation, I tell them what I do and it produces business.

Chapter Eleven

My Perfect Day

Once you have developed My Big Why and feel drawn into the vision it supplies, keeping it in front of you all the time, then you can best bring it to pass by enthusiastically embracing every day as an opportunity to make it happen. Each of us can design the outline of My Perfect Day built around both our work and non-work activities.

So each day, for example, we need to be asking questions of ourselves about what should we focus on this day—at this moment. With respect to our real estate careers, the development and support of our client relationships are critically important. But it is also important to set aside time in each day to learn new things and acquire new skills. In our personal lives, we need to maintain and enhance the relationships we have with important people. But in addition we also must set aside time to give back to our community and focus on our own personal health and welfare.

So My Perfect Day includes active engagement in my business, but also active engagement with my wife and children, other loved ones and friends. And it involves ways I am privileged to give back to my community as well as exercising, proper diet and other health-related endeavors.

You can outline on one 8" x 11" piece of paper every evening as you plan your next day to make sure you attend to each important thing in your life. Every night look at the outline and make sure that tomorrow you're getting those things done.

Eventually, My Perfect Day can become a routine. The longest living people on earth are those who have adopted and maintained healthy and productive routines. I encourage people to do that.

Presented here are the stories of several agents who have made My Perfect Day an important part of their lives. The first one is from Tim Rhode, who taught it to me.

∽

TIM RHODE
'Days when the good guys win'
(More insights from Tim are in Chapters Six and Nine.)

To best describe My Perfect Day, I need to give an overview picture of what that means for me. In my mind, we're not talking about a perfect day; we're talking about the vision of a happy, healthy and productive life that is lived to one's fullest.

It starts with a long-term vision of where you see yourself down the road: My Big Why. [See Chapter Six for Tim Rhode's thoughts on My Big Why.] You can only talk about My Perfect Day in the context of what it means in relation to long-term planning.

In order to get to what My Perfect Day is, it is best if we have this long-term plan of where we see ourselves many years down the road. At age 40, when all of this started, I wrote out a portrait of myself for when I am age 95. I also wrote out where I saw myself at 65, which was then 25 years into the future. But my main vision plan was my 10-year plan. That was the plan I used as a feeder to connect with my one-year, monthly, weekly and perfect day plans.

Here's a good analogy: How do you drive to Detroit? Do you just jump in your car and start driving? No, you MapQuest it, which tells you how to get on this freeway and that roadway so eventually you end up in Detroit. What I'm talking about here is MapQuesting your trip to Detroit, except it's about writing down what you're going to do with your trip through life, which studies show fewer than 3 percent of the people do.

This process is going to take some time. You're going to struggle a bit. But please stay with it. I'm here to tell you it's worth the effort—and so are you.

After writing out my 10-year plan, I wrote out my one-year plan and used it to update my 10-year plan, making corrections as needed. Then every month, at the end of the month, I critiqued the month just past and wrote out my following month's plan, including every area of my life, to ensure I'm in balance and not falling off somewhere else.

When doing my annual plan, I'd look at my 10-year plan. When doing my monthly plan, I'd look at my yearly plan. And when doing my weekly plan, I'd look at my monthly plan. Every now and then I'd find stuff that kept getting carried over for months at a time and realized these items really weren't that important. If I had an item on the list for seven months and hadn't done anything about it, I'd tell myself, "I'm not going to either. And that's okay."

Each year I also rated myself on each of the different circles of balance that made up my "Life Wheel." If I am low in one area, I make allowances. One year my wife and I talked and realized we didn't have very many friends; we didn't do much stuff with other people. It led us to create a group of four couples. We get together to play cards, go out, go on vacations and watch our families grow.

Every week, on a Sunday afternoon or evening, I would write out my plan for that week and critique the preceding week. Then, every morning I'd take that weekly plan and make out a daily plan, a plan for a perfect day.

If there was time at the end of the day, I'd look at the daily plan, mark off the things that got done, carry over the things that didn't get done to tomorrow and add on new items I wanted to get accomplished or people I needed to call or see. If I couldn't finish all of it that night, I'd get to it first thing in the morning.

It takes an extra five or 10 minutes a day to do this. I found it invaluable. I also made a game out of it and made it fun along the way, always striving to achieve the perfect day.

I had My Perfect Day sheeting, my daily activity log. On it was the date, my calls, my to-do list, my to-see list, how many hours I planned to work that day, how many dollar productive hours there would be (in my mind, that means I'm either with a qualified client who can buy or sell real estate or I'm actively prospecting for somebody who might buy or sell a listing), how many contacts I was going to talk to that day, how many appointments I was going on that day, how many listings I was going to take, how many sales I would do that day and also whether I exercised and ate right that day. (Note that I only worked with sellers. Real estate agents typically should also have a sheet on how many buyer showing appointments they expect to do.)

If I properly covered all of the areas on the sheet in a single day, I got to circle the words "Perfect Day" that were printed at the bottom. I always have a game going with myself. So on the days I get to circle Perfect Day, the good guys have won.

I figure that I get to circle Perfect Day four days a month. I find it's best to focus on my efforts, not on my results. You can only control your efforts; you can't force the results. For example, you can't make someone sign a contract—unless you have a big gun. Just kidding.

In addition, I had a sheet I'd compile called "Tim's Monthly Stats." For each month of the year, it had separate columns covering days worked, calls made, appointments held, listings, offers, listing sales, buyer sales, Tim sales and closings. (I had other agents working for me who worked buyer leads.) What I focused on was how many days I would work, how many calls and door-knocks I would make that would lead me to how many appointments, which would lead to so many listings. I found if I just focused on the days worked, calls, contacts and appointments, the rest would fall into place. Again, I can't control the results; I can only control my efforts and my mindset—my disposition. I am walking into the appointment absolutely convinced I'm getting the listing. The client has to talk me out of not listing the home for the proper price and with a listing that gives enough time to get the job done at a full commission.

For instance, in 1999, my monthly stats showed I worked an average of 16 days a month, which means I had great balance. Most people worked many more days a week and many more hours per day than me. But where I excelled was spending a higher percentage of my time being dollar productive—time spent either prospecting or face-to-face with bona fide decision makers. I made an average of 563 calls a month. I went on an average of 37 listing appointments a month. I took an average of 16 listings a month. I produced an average of 25 offers a month. An average of 15 of my listings went pending per month. We closed an average of 12 deals a month.

It's very important to only work with motivated, qualified people. I never worked with buyers, but if I did they would not set foot in my car if they weren't pre-qualified, motivated and ready to buy. I only took listings that were priced right and showed well for the price. I didn't take over-priced listings or work with non-motivated clients. I think this served me well, not only in getting more paychecks, but also in having less aggravation and stress in my life. Once, when I told a prospective seller, "I'm proud of the fact I've never been sued," he replied, "You've never worked with me." At that point, I looked him in the eyes and said, "I won't be working with you," got up and walked away from the appointment. Life is too short for that kind of aggravation.

~

ROSA GONZALEZ
'Keeping focused and on track'
(Also catch more from Rosa in Chapters Two, Three, Six and Nine.)

I had a schedule. I did pretty much what I saw Jerry Katzakian do.

He was the real estate agent I worked for before becoming an agent myself. First thing, I sent cards out and let everyone I knew know I was in real estate. I had used the list of people from the school where I worked for 10 years, including the names and phone numbers of every parent, in addition to my direct sphere of influence—people I know and who know me.

I'd make phone calls in the morning, prospect expired listings and for-sale-by-owners—and just anyone I knew. I set up a system to make sure I was in touch with them once a month through phone calling and in-person stopping by.

I did some element of training every day: learning how to answer the phone, listening to CDs by entrepreneurs and real estate trainers. Then, if I wasn't showing a property to a prospective buyer, I was previewing properties, opening and closing deals, processing the file, doing the paperwork, talking to title and escrow people, other agents and clients, and building on my database by using referrals from past clients.

I'd also state my affirmations out loud every morning while preparing for the day: "I'm a powerful real estate agent. I'm here to teach and encourage. My day will be fun."

Of course, they're not the same every day. It's whatever is going on in my head at the time—but all just positive affirmations.

Before going to the office, every day I talk with my accountability partner. For three years, Phil Watson and I have been constant accountability partners. He's a real estate agent for more than 30 years in San Bruno, in the Bay Area. Talking with him twice a day—at the beginning and end of the day—is one of the most consistent things I do.

We talk about what our goals are for the day, the appointments we have set up and what we're trying to achieve today. We can discuss anything new we learned the day before, how we talked to a negotiator on a deal; we share what we learn from each other. This is a very two-way exchange. Then, at the end of the day how did that appointment go? Did we get the listing? What would we have done different? Oh, and we always remind ourselves to remember to laugh, to smile.

What I get out of it is keeping me on task, keeping me focused. He encourages me every day and I do the same for him. We both keep moving forward. There are times when he says he feels like this business is really getting to him. Then we talk and he's rejuvenated.

For the last three years I've been part of the Bay Area Mastermind Group, real estate agents in the greater San Francisco Bay Area. My accountability partner is one of them too. We all get together in person at least twice a year. But every last Friday of the month we have a conference call. There are eight of us. We share ideas, what we're doing in today's market, what are our achievements, what we learned not to do, what computers and databases are we using now.

My business started to grow. I made more than 20 deals the first year. In 2004 and 2005, I increased my numbers. There was only one year in that decade when my numbers didn't go up.

When the market started to change in 2006, I turned to short sales. In the beginning there were clients who already knew me and unfortunately had to do short sales. I helped them out.

My database is truly made up of referrals. Ninety percent of all my clients are referrals. In 2006, my clientele was not only from referrals, but also from referrals by other agents in my own industry who were referring to me because they knew I was specializing in short sales and they trusted me. Not many agents want to do short sales. Many think it's too much work and the possibility of closing deals is not that great. So you can end up doing a whole lot of work for nothing.

The paperwork is a lot more complicated and involved. It takes longer. The biggest thing is the unknown because you don't know if the transaction is going to get approved by the lender or note-holder.

I'm still doing short sales. You have to be careful and diligent. The most important thing about short sales is communication. My philosophy I developed in 2006 was compassion. That takes being present with the person and truly understanding what he or she is going through. I try to tell myself it's me. I take what they're telling me and tell myself that I could be in their shoes. Sometimes I really hear and listen to what is not being said so I can achieve the goal of expressing through the hardship letter or when I get to talk with the negotiator for the lender that this is not just a hardship; this is somebody who has been through some crisis: lost a job, gone through a divorce—or just hit hard times.

That helps a lot in dealing with the negotiators. When they package a short sale to present to the decision maker, if the whole package is correctly put together and there is a reason for the hardship, then the chances for closing the short sale are increased.

Beginning in 2009, most of my business came from bank-owned properties and this continues to be so. The opportunities just came along.

I definitely work with buyers, representing them with my team of five people. I have a full-time assistant, a part-time assistant, two short sale team members who are real estate agents and a buyers' specialist, representing buyers with me.

I'm pretty diversified: I do short sales, bank-owned sales and some traditional sales with people who still have equity in their homes. I make an effort to keep in contact with my sphere of influence.

Diversifying is important. A real estate coach in 2008 was coaching me, and one of the most important things he told me is that so many people in the '90s economy—when there was a similar situation with lots of short sales and bank-owned properties—would focus primarily on what would bring in the money at the time. The biggest lesson learned from that period is, yes, you have to work with what's out there, but you also have to be diversified because if you focus on only one part of the market, when the market changes, and it will change, you're left with nothing.

～

MIKE BAZUIK
'Defining my time better'
(You can check out more from Mike in Chapters Two, Six and Nine.)

I've watched Tim Rhode work. He really has it together. I want to define my time better—prospect and do less paperwork. I have an escrow coordinator now who frees up a fair amount of my time. I like to come in like Tim, prospect for three hours, get lunch and come back and do presentations in the afternoons—and that's it. Then go home. It's a schedule where you're working aggressively but have a crew that handles much of the work so your job is less time-consuming and more focused.

Right now, I grab whatever I can get. If it's a buyer lead, I'm going to show that buyer property. If it's a short sale, I'm going try to get the short sale. If it's a bank sending me a listing, I'm going to accept the listing and move forward with it. If I go to a trust deed sale and buy the flipper property, then it's making the improvements or repairs and selling for the biggest possible profit.

About the Author

Michael P. Zagaris was born and raised in California's Central Valley. He received his B.A. degree in economics with honors from the University of California, Santa Cruz, and his Masters in Business Administration from Santa Clara University.

Prior to joining his family's real estate business in 1977, Zagaris worked in management positions at Xidex Corporation in Sunnyvale, California, and Memphis, Tennessee, as well as ALZA Corporation in Palo Alto.

He presently serves as president and CEO of PMZ Real Estate. In addition, he is president of Zagaris Management Services, a family-owned land development firm, and chairman of Scenic Oaks Funding, a family-owned mortgage banking company. He is chairman of Directline Technologies in Modesto, a leading nationwide provider of telemarketing services for colleges, universities and nonprofit organizations. He is co-founder and co-owner of CentralValleyJobs. com, the leading online job site in the Central Valley.

In addition, Zagaris has been actively involved in many nonprofit and community activities. He has served as president of the California State University, Stanislaus Foundation, president of the State Theatre of Modesto, chairman of the Doctors Medical Center Board of Governors and co-founder of the Leadership Modesto program.

Mike Zagaris lives with his wife, Midge, in Modesto. Their five children are grown and they are now enjoying their grandchildren.

He can be contacted at 209-548-4510 or at mzagaris@pmz.com.

About PMZ Real Estate

PMZ Real Estate is the largest provider of real estate services in Central California. Paul M. Zagaris, who began his real estate career in 1947 in Modesto, founded the company. This family-run independent real estate firm is now owned by Paula Zagaris Leffler, Jon Zagaris and Michael Zagaris.

With annual sales of well over $1 billion, PMZ Real Estate is among the top 50 real estate companies in the United States. It provides residential brokerage, commercial/industrial brokerage and property management services.

Additional information is available at www.pmz.com.